# MY HARVARD
# PORTFOLIO

# MY HARVARD PORTFOLIO

How 30 Harvard Students (and the Parents)
Built their Portfolios from Ground Zero

JIYOON KIM

# A NOTE TO MY READERS:

*My Harvard Portfolio* gives students and parents personal, academic, and admission insight from 30 Harvard students and alumni.

This book was originally intended for the South Korean audience, but I received such positive feedback from our readers in America that I decided to publish the English version first. Although all of these interviewees are Korean by heritage, I believe that with any personal story, there is a universal message or messages within each given story we can all relate to.

The interviews are written and transcribed in their most "raw" state as much as possible—the words they used during the actual interview combined with some of their written answers from preliminary surveys. The color of their voice and personality is what makes each profile distinct from one another.

# DEDICATION & ACKNOWLEDGEMENTS:

This collection of interviews is dedicated to all students who felt like a school of their dreams was out of reach. I want to let them know that all of these students and alumni from Harvard are just like you, and with effort and determination, you can make it too.

To my family, who lovingly raised me and taught me everything I know. To my in-laws, who support me with everything that I do. To my little boy Eli, who is my everything.

I want to thank all of these people below who made this book possible. From helping me revise the content, checking for grammatical errors, and giving me constructive feedback and ideas for the book, I am so grateful for the help. *My Harvard Portfolio* **would not be possible without you guys.**

Thank you Soomin Chun, Michelle Chung, Dongkeun Han, Joon Yeop Kim, Annie Nam, and Alyssa Suh.

# FOREWORD:

*At the buffet line and why I wrote this book.*

When you first arrive at the Bellagio Hotel dinner buffet in Las Vegas, you are overwhelmed.

No one tells you to be prepared for the carousel of dishes once you step inside. It's an explosive color palette for your eyes—but you can't look away. You stare at the seafood ceviche, the leg of lamb, the piles of boiled snow crabs, the basket of fresh lemons and limes, the assortment of steamed dim sum, then momentarily admire the extravagant flower arrangements engulfing the room in the best way possible. You hold your empty plate in your hand and get out of line to compose yourself. Let's not mention the display of desserts. That's for another time.

This is how I felt when I first stepped foot on Harvard's campus when I was twelve-years-old making the typical early-bird college road trip with the family and again as a masters student at the Harvard Graduate School of Education.

Harvard was the Bellagio dinner buffet of universities.

I was utterly overwhelmed by the glow of pride and history radiating from Harvard students' faces that no New England freezing winter could extinguish. Everyone was walking with purpose.

Something that told me that these extraordinary, inspiring, and hardworking individuals—nearly superheroes in the eyes of a twelve-year-old—who managed to gain admission to one of the most prestigious and famous universities in the world, were also just like everyone else. Kids who in the past needed their nightlight to sleep or were class clowns in school. Students who wrote a decade's worth of dreams and plans in journals but who also felt lost too along the way. I was keen to know their journeys to find these universals.

What better way to show students and families out there then to personally interview Harvard students about the pathway they carved with their families to get to where they are now.

So, I interviewed 30 Harvard students and alumni, asking them a list of questions about their personal and academic journey to Harvard. Each interview lasted about an hour each, and I wish I could have put everything they said in this book. But alas, each student profile would then exceed 70 pages. The interviewees didn't have to answer some questions if they didn't have the answer for it or didn't want to. Some gave lengthy answers to some questions, others a shorter response. Thus, My Harvard Portfolio **was born.**

Pay attention to how, at times, these students made complete pivots along the way or how they best utilized their surrounding resources to explore their interests. Pay attention to how these individuals' parents supported them. Whether it was staying past midnight to help them solve math problems or encouraged them in everything that seemed interesting to their child—may it be collecting rocks or holding theatrical plays for the family.

This book may help you get into the college you have always dreamed of attending.

# CONTENTS:

## Harvard College

## Harvard Graduate and Professional

# A Quick Overview of Our Harvard Interviewees

15 Students from Harvard College
15 Students from Harvard Graduate and Professional Schools
17 Female Students
13 Male Students
18 International Students
12 U.S.A Students

## Harvard College Majors Represented

Bioengineering
Biological Sciences
Comparative Literature
Computer Science
Economics
German
Government
History
Integrative Biology
Linguistics
Music
Philosophy
Public Health
Social Studies
Theater, Dance, Media (TDM)

## Harvard Graduate and Professional Schools Represented

Harvard Business School
Harvard Graduate School of Design
Harvard Graduate School of Education
Harvard Kennedy School
Harvard Law School
Harvard Medical School
Harvard T.H. Chan School of Public Health

# HARVARD COLLEGE

# The Software Engineer & Basketball Kid

## David Jeong

**Education:**
Harvard College, AB Computer Science, Class of 2017
Nutley High School, Rank (2/375)

**GPA and Test Scores:**
GPA, (Weighted (4.80/5.1), Unweighted (3.91/4.0))
SAT I, (2340, (Math: 800, Reading: 750, Writing: 790))
SAT II, (Math II (800), Physics (790))
APs, (Calculus BC, English Language and Composition, English Literature and Composition, Spanish Language and Culture, Chemistry, Biology, Physics I, Physics C: Mechanics, Physics C: Electricity and Magnetism)
Grades, (A- to A+ throughout all subjects (one B+ in one quartile))

**Extracurriculars and Awards:**
Basketball : 4 years (3 years varsity), Track & Field Long Jump/Triple Jump: (4 years varsity), Chamber Choir: 4 years, New Jersey All-State Choir: 3 years, US All-Eastern Choir: 1 year, Marching Band - Saxophone: 2 years, Musical Theater: 2 years, Spanish Honor Society-President: 1 year (3 years total)

Essex County Academic Excellence Award, Essex County Math Competition-Calculus 2nd Place, Salutatorian of Nutley High School, Academic Excellence Scholarship at Nutley High School, Academic Excellence Scholarship at Nutley High School.

**Hometown:**
Nutley, NJ, Busan, South Korea

*What are your quirks? What do you think makes you unique?*

Being able to discern what I want to pursue versus what others in the world want me to pursue. I always feel happy and confident because I continuously ask myself what I actually want. Sometimes that means working the whole day and other times that means rolling around in bed for a week straight. Let happiness be the driving force in your decisions!

*1. What kind of child were you growing up, and what were your interests?*

Obsessive. That's the single word that defined my childhood. I pursued even the smallest interests. I actually traded and sold collectible cards with collectors across the world in elementary school. I used to walk to the post office every day to send and receive cards. I took this very seriously too. I'd take activities that my friends considered as little hobbies to another level and devote my full attention to them. In 6th grade, I even ended up in Pittsburgh to compete in a national Yu-Gi-Oh card game tournament.

I was also really fascinated with stuff that I wasn't good at. I tried out for the 6th grade Boys and Girls Club basketball team and didn't make the cut. It definitely hurt, but I kind of appreciated the fact that when you're terrible at something, there is a lot of chance for improvement. Besides schoolwork, by no means of exaggeration, I started practicing basketball eight hours a day for two years straight to prove to myself that I could one day play on the high school basketball team. I ended up playing on the varsity team for three years in high school.

Most of these obsessions didn't benefit my academic performance or my resume. In fact, they probably hurt my scores here and there, but that was always okay with me, as long as I had something exciting to look forward to every single day. If I were to answer the question "what was your childhood interest," my best one-word response would be "excitement." I chased whatever thrilled me.

*2. How involved were your parents in helping you to prepare for Harvard? How did they help you to learn and grow?*

My parents were quite removed from my academic development, in a traditional sense. They rarely asked to see my grades and didn't force me to study. This was partially because they did not speak English very well and could not afford the cost of extra studies as poor immigrants. They also thought they weren't qualified enough to help me with my school material. I started to develop a habit of googling everything or searching things I didn't know. I realized there were so many free resources online. Despite being disadvantaged socio-economically or having parents with a language barrier, I was able to find answers to questions I had. At one point, I remember I wanted to attend academies like my other friends and my mom said she would be willing to take out loans so that I can attend SAT or science academies. That was when I realized I really have to study and figure things out on my own because I didn't want to be the one bringing more financial burdens on the family.

I think the biggest thing for me was that my parents always told me that they were confident in my decisions. From early on, my mom half-jokingly asked me for my take on what she should do about her dilemmas and would often demonstrate how an adult thinks instead of teaching it to me. I was aware of what my mom was thinking and what adults were thinking about. I felt motivated by the fact that grown-ups trusted me. If I wanted to join a club or go to an event, they were confident that I had weighed the pros and cons of my actions, so it was very rare to get an unreasonable "no."

My parents wanted to see me become a good person before a successful person, but the irony was I grew up wanting to succeed and make them proud.

*3. What is your most memorable memory in preparation for Harvard, and what was something you experienced that you never thought you ever would?*

I come from a slightly below average public high school in New Jersey. I had counselors who doubted that you could get into these top schools since, generally speaking, even the top students at my high school were unsuccessful at getting into top schools. Being in a school system like that for four years, you almost develop an expectation to *not* get into a school like Harvard. I was genuinely shocked to receive my acceptance letter.

And while I wouldn't necessarily encourage others to abandon hope, not carrying heavy burdens on my shoulders actually helped me quite a bit, to be honest. I was not as stressed as my peers, which I think also boosted my academic performance.

In hindsight, if you are a hard-working and smart student, you are generally going to do well wherever you go, and the best way to prepare to get into the top schools is not to pressure yourself. Don't lock yourself into one or two schools but be open-ended. There are dozens and dozens of great schools. I guess more specifically if I'm going to be a little bit more practical and if you are aiming for Harvard, there's no way to sugarcoat it—you definitely have to do a lot in order to do well. You have to recognize that some of the most talented kids are preparing in their own ways to go to this school. And while you shouldn't try to kill yourself with school and extracurriculars, but there should be some sort of push and a level of grit that you need.

*4. Study tips you have for younger students.*

Ironically my study tip is something that I learned while playing basketball, which may seem far removed from studying. In sports we have a lot of strategies—the coaches draw X's and O's so you move this way and that way. While my teammates were (not to offend them in any way) not the top students in our school, they would learn the strategies incredibly fast and memorize the moves so quickly. And I realized that if you can find a way to enjoy something and actually care about it, you'll learn really fast—and that's the best way to learn.

So, applying this in an academic sense, certain subjects may seem difficult, but practice enjoying what you are learning. At the same time, don't feel like you're being cornered into anything and if you feel the pressure from parents or school, while it may depend on the parent-student relationship, I think it's important that you tell your parents that you're feeling stressed and overworked.

*5. What do you believe was your "X" factor to gain an admission to Harvard?*

I think my essay and various non-academic extracurriculars were the biggest factors. My essay was centered on my positive obsession on whatever I fell in love with. I did not feel the need to sugarcoat any achievements or boast about some grand feat. I also didn't want my South Korean heritage or immigrant status to be my "diversity factor" in the eyes of the college admissions. Like I had mentioned, I had put in 8 hours of basketball every single day for almost a thousand days. So I wanted that level of obsession to be a distinguishing trait.

As for the extracurriculars, I was involved in a lot of clubs and organizations, performed choral music at a national level, played varsity basketball and track & field. Oddly enough, I did not have a single academic extracurricular throughout high school. I didn't realize that this was unusual until I got to Harvard and heard about other students' experiences with debate teams, math Olympiads, and so on. I would like to loosely borrow the words of one of my college academic advisors: "Shouldn't having great grades in school be enough for academics? There's more to a student than just studying. I'd rather accept a good student who has felt the physical grit of a sports team and mental challenge of a gaming club than a good student who has just studied more."

While I graduated as the salutatorian of my school, I don't think my grades could have been the 'X factor' because I came from a below-average public high school in America. Even the top students at my school every year were considered lucky to get accepted to one high tier school.

*6. What are some of the challenges you have faced in school?*

The biggest challenge coming to Harvard was that I lacked significant resources.

When I was applying to colleges, I didn't have someone in the family who could help me with the process. Most of my friends had parents who would know how to fill out financial applications, but I had to figure those things out myself. While other students could focus solely on school, I was helping out my mom and my dad with whatever they needed help with due to their language barrier, especially with things like legal paperwork. And there were even times when we were struggling financially, so I had to save money in not so pleasant ways. There were times where we had to ration meals to save money. But I am incredibly lucky, in a sense, to be born with a positive attitude. I never considered my circumstances to be devastating or sad. Part of this stems from my having a younger brother and younger sister, and I was always being aware that whatever they did may not affect me that much, but my actions would significantly affect them.

At Harvard, it took a bit of adjusting to fit in. Academically, students who came from private schools or international schools seemed like they were well prepared—in fact, most of my friends claim that their high school was more challenging than Harvard. This was a very common thing that I've heard, but this wasn't the case for me. In the early years, I definitely found the classes a little bit difficult. Other students had spent significant time away from home and knew what to do right away–especially those kids who used to attend boarding schools. I think I was so preoccupied trying to adjust to everything, and I only realized the importance of cultivating meaningful friendships in my junior year or so.

*7. What do you find most valuable about your Harvard education?*

There's a lot of stigma or assumptions out there about Harvard College. When I started I did not know a single person growing up who had gone to Harvard, so I had no idea what to expect. I had read stuff online and heard rumors—you hear a lot of scary stuff out there. But one thing I can definitely say for sure having gone through the Harvard experience is that your Harvard education is not overrated.

Classes are great, but they're probably no different from any other top school if I had to guess. What I found most interesting about Harvard were conversations I had with people. The school has a culture of fostering meaningful discussions all the time. And I don't mean this in the sense of an important class that leads to an intellectually stimulating conversation. As soon as you get to your first-year, the second, third, or fourth-year students are always pushing you to think about something. They want to meet up with you to discuss what you had said earlier, and they want to sit down with you while eating lunch to discuss some points that we had talked about the previous day. In fact, it will be extremely hard to go to this school and not think about yourself as a person and how you can change as a person. And while I noticed that a lot of my friends obviously prioritized school, grades, and internships, for so many of my friends, the thing that was on top of their minds all the time was in fact, "Am I growing as a person and introspecting enough?" I think this is something that people might be surprised to find out about Harvard students. I think that's really the most powerful thing about the university's education.

The school's flexible academic curriculum also assisted fostering self-exploration. Harvard is very willing to show students flexibility—if you have an educational interest that you want to explore, the school will more often than not, simply ask you to submit your own major. In fact, Harvard is constantly encouraging you to take some quirky classes and pursue random things you are interested in. The flexibility ensures that you have room in your schedule to do so.

*8. What are you currently doing now or plan on doing in the future?*

I initially entered Harvard as a mechanical engineering/physics major. Not really for any particularly good reason other than those were the subjects that I was good at in high school. About a year-and-a-half, maybe, two years into mechanical engineering, one requirement course I had to take was computer science. I found it kind of exciting and wanted to change my major. And to this day I'm working as a software developer, still in that 'obsession' phase, trying to better my skills. I make iPhone apps, iPad apps, and work for various companies. I currently work for Barstool Sports and have previously worked for ESPN and Disney.

My plan for the future is pretty simple. My friends have really big goals that they want to achieve and high positions that they want to attain, but my plans are just to be as independent from my job and my finances as much as possible. Gaining the freedom and not being controlled by my job or money is what I'm hoping for. Having a family and providing for them is another goal of mine.

*Summary of Key Points:*

1. For Students: Don't let the things you're not good at in the beginning get you down. There's only room for improvement from there.
2. For Parents: Trust that your children also know how to make a decision for their future.
3. Never feel disheartened by your lack of resources or poor financial standing. By keeping a positive outlook, you can overcome the shortcomings and achieve a goal of yours.

*Review:*

David's story is inspirational and has universal messages that a lot of people can relate to. He's someone who has overcome so many systematic difficulties and yet speaks very positively about his experiences. Instead of complaining about not having enough to eat to save money, he sees it as an opportunity to become a role model for his younger siblings and give back to others like him. He reminds everyone that you should never despair but to remember that there is always a way out in the end.

# The Biologist & the Iron-Willed Football Player

## Benjamin Chun

**Education:**
Harvard College, Integrative Biology, Class of 2022
Nanuet Senior High School, Class Valedictorian

**GPA and Test Scores:**
GPA, (102.34%)
SAT I, (1530 (Math 800, Reading 730))
SAT II, (Biology (800), Math 2 (800))
APs, (Calculus AB, English Language and Composition, English Literature and Composition, Environmental Science, European History, U.S. History)

**Extracurriculars and Awards:**
Captain of Nanuet Varsity Football Team, Captain of the Varsity Tennis Team, Study Body President, Captain of the Nanuet Community Ambulance Youth Corps, Vice President of the Model U.N. Club, Captain of the Science Olympiad Club, Concertmaster of the Nanuet Chamber Orchestra, Commissioner of Sustainability and Economic Development at N.Y. Boys' State, Captain of the Nanuet Debate Team, Coordinator of a Mentorship Program for young musicians ("Big Musicians"), research intern at the Charles Meshul Laboratory

Bausch + Lomb Honorary Science Award, National Merit Scholarship Finalist, Rockland-Scholar Athlete

**Hometown:**
Nanuet, New York

*What are your quirks? What do you think makes you unique?*

I don't know if this is a quirk, but something I have to do every day is to work out for at least an hour. My routine started at the beginning of high school, and it's been a consistent thing every day.

*1. What kind of child were you growing up, and what were your interests?*

When I was a kid, I was never really passionate about anything. I started playing the violin in third grade, but I mostly stayed indoors and kept to myself since I was bullied a lot in school, and it was really hard for me to make friends. I was an overweight kid and one of the very few Asian students in my grade, so I used video games as my "escape" from reality. I played a lot of League of Legends, Call of Duty, Warcraft—you name it. Since both of my parents worked full-time, they weren't really aware of what was going on with me, and I had a nanny for most of my childhood years.

Then, at the beginning of high school, that's when everything changed for me because my dad started working from home and noticed that I needed a lot of support and help. Then, my parents recommended I try out for sports to make friends. I really wanted to play football, but it was the one sport my mom was against since she considered it extremely dangerous. It took about two months of back and forth arguments and reasoning with my family, but they finally decided to let me join because it was that one thing I really wanted to do for myself. I think my mom realized at some point that if I joined any other sport, I would just quit right away, so she agreed in the end despite the possibility of broken bones and torn ligaments. I wanted to join the school team for two reasons, really. One, because I saw that if many obese people like me could play, I could do it too. And two, I know this sounds really evil, but a lot of my bullies were on the football team and I kind of wanted to get back at them in some way. I remember during the first few practices, my coach would have to throw me out because I would start fistfights with my teammates.

Oddly enough, after just one season when we started winning together and building bonds, I became best friends with my former bullies towards the end of high school.

*2. How involved were your parents in helping you to prepare for Harvard? How did they help you to learn and grow?*

Like I said before, my parents were so worried that I would get injured while playing football, but in the end, I had their full support after they saw me getting healthier and making friends. They came to every game, drove me to every practice, and even drove me to the gym every morning before school started. In many instances, I struggled a lot with managing my time between football, violin, and schoolwork, but one of the most important skills I learned from my parents was micromanaging my time. So basically every year, they bought me a planner and showed me how I have to split up my day into specific hours and what had to get done within each hour. And because of that, I kept up with it all through high school and it honestly really helped. If I didn't complete that task within the hour, I felt really crappy about it.

As for my preparation for Harvard, they both didn't really have the school in mind. My dream school was West Point, and my dad always wanted me to go to West Point since he loved everything about it, especially the free tuition. My mom agreed with him as well but still wanted me to apply to the Ivies. I actually didn't look at other schools until the fall of my senior year. I've also been training to get into West Point since the ninth grade by getting in shape for the CFA Test, which is a lot of pull-ups and push-ups and focusing on leadership roles. So, when I got my early acceptance letter from West Point, my mom suggested that I also apply to Harvard to see what happens. And then, yeah, so I was never really preparing for Harvard, but I was preparing for West Point, and my Harvard acceptance just happened. I remember there were clashes every day between my dad and mom on which school I should attend. Dad was still for West Point, but Mom had switched sides to Harvard. In the end, I wanted to become a doctor and had to ask myself if I wanted to become an army doctor or one for the general masses. I figured it was a lot more challenging to get into medical school if I graduated from West Point, and not only that, Harvard offered the networking opportunities and social life that West Point couldn't. Harvard won.

*3. What is your most memorable memory in preparation for Harvard, and what was something you experienced that you never thought you ever would?*

When I got my early acceptance letter for West Point, everything was so calm for me. Then, suddenly, I was applying to Harvard last-minute in the fall, and that's when things got hectic for me. It was a pretty busy time that fall, too, because I had major debate competitions, major football championships and all that was on my plate. But in the end, I think that whole hectic time worked out for me in the end because I was able to win certain competitions and championships and send in those accomplishments into the portal even after applications were due. There was a section where you could upload supplementary material, so I think that helped a lot. During this whole application process, another memorable experience was sitting down and writing my personal statements for both Harvard and West Point. I took the time to think about what helped me to transform as a person. It made me appreciate not only my family but my identity as well. So the whole process was very cathartic for me. I ended up writing my personal statement about my bullying experience and how, in the end, through football, we became best friends. We always joke now on how they actually used to throw me into the lockers. Yeah, but it's a old joke now.

*4. Study tips you have for younger students.*

So, I think that number one is micromanaging your time either with a planner or post-it note and writing out what you will do in your day's specific time slots. The other thing that helped me was writing out my notes. Many of my classmates typed out their notes, but I didn't learn anything from typing for me. In terms of taking tests like the SAT, the most crucial thing was repeatedly taking practice tests. I was doing them three to four times a day. Even if you think it's useless after just taking one, it is not, because only by repetition will you get to know the types of questions. For your regular school classes, if you can sit down with your classmate or friend and explain and teach concepts to them, then the material becomes finalized in your head. If I had to do high school over again and change one thing, it would be to drop the clubs I wasn't that serious about or trying to get leadership positions in. I shouldn't have joined a club just because I thought it would be a "resume builder." Many clubs that I was involved in, now looking back, it was honestly a waste of time for me. I should have stuck to the main clubs that I was really liking.

*5. What do you believe was your "X" factor to gain admission to Harvard?*

I think being the captain of a sport that not many Koreans play was what set me apart. When I read my admission file, they touched upon my organizational skills on how I managed football, then jump to violin practice, and then to work—things that were completely different from one another. Also, I think the fact that barely any Asians play football made me stand out in a way. There was also this section within your admissions file where, during your interview, they grade you numerically on things I didn't expect to be evaluated on, such as the flow of conversation, my critical-thinking skills, etc. Everything in this section was on a scale of 1 to5. Some notes within the file said things like, "This part of his application is good, but we need to rely on the interview." So definitely sports, my leadership positions, and my interview helped me get in.

*6. What are some of the challenges you have faced in school?*

I think challenge-wise, college coursework is very different from high school coursework. For me, it's just a lot more information at one time. I had to change my study habits and focus on micromanaging my time. At the start of my freshman year at Harvard, I tried to do what I did in high school and join every club. I even wanted to join seven different clubs of my own. Please don't do what I did. No one can survive that way. So lately, in my sophomore year, I figured out that wasn't the right way to do it, so I dropped like five clubs and I'm focusing on two to three now. In terms of making friends, since I grew up in a majority white neighborhood, when I first arrived at Harvard, it was just so diverse in terms of the people and I didn't feel up to par with that diversity. So it was even difficult for me to fit into the Korean and Korean American community at Harvard at first. But right now, I found my family and community in the Korean Association and have really connected with everybody.

*7. What do you find most valuable about your Harvard education?*

When people ask me this, I always have the same answer because I find that I get asked this a lot. I break it up, usually into three main things. One, definitely the professors. For example, I had a poetry class that I had to take to fulfill an arts and humanities requirement, and the course was on *Paradise Lost* by John Milton. I later found out halfway that my professor was the person who edited the workload, and we're studying his work, and the poetry was just crazy in general. After that class, for some odd reason, I really got into poetry. Two, the resources available. There are just so many things specifically for each major, and for me, since I'm taking a lot of biology classes, all the labs are absolutely pristine. There was a deep-sea biology class I was taking, and we took the R.V. into the Charles River to simulate the machine exploring the ocean. Three, the diverse group of people you will meet there. Since Harvard stresses group work, you just meet so many people that way and make close friends that way. And everyone changes and challenges your perspective in the best way possible. That's the beauty of my education there. This is also a bonus, but there are just so many classes here that you wouldn't even think of. There's a class on clowns, like the theory of clowns, and another class on chocolate and wine. There's something for everybody here.

*8. What are you currently doing now or plan on doing in the future?*

So, right now, I'm taking this organic chemistry class that I want to get out of the way, but I fulfilled all of my Pre-Med requirements besides the physics course load this coming year. After my senior year ends, later on, I might take a gap year to apply to different medical schools and do some research work. I am not sure yet. But I do know I want to be a surgeon later on. For me, I wanted to become a doctor after watching *Grey's Anatomy*. I just really wanted to help people. My dad, a CPA accountant, always said if he had the chance to go back, he would study medicine. My mom is a dentist, and she says she never gets respect as a dentist and would much rather have me be a doctor. If possible, I want to be an orthopedic surgeon for a major football team and just travel all over the world with the team. That's my dream job.

*Summary of Key Points:*

1. For Students: Don't join every club in the entire world. Select a few and dedicate your time to the ones you enjoy.
2. For Parents: Help your children micromanage their time. Break up their days into time slots and what they will achieve during those periods.
3. Keep in mind that sometimes your enemies will not remain your enemies forever. People grow and change, and new friendships start to heal the wounds from the past.

*Review:*

Benjamin has made quite the transformation from an introverted child who got bullied in school to an all-star athlete, academic, and aspiring surgeon who has the discipline to accomplish his goals in the most organized way possible. He even became best friends with his childhood bullies, the very same people who threw Benjamin into lockers like they do in the movies. What is striking is that once his dad started working from home and noticed how Benjamin needed a lot of support, his life and mindset changed for the better. It may seem like a small change to some, but the impact was significant in Benjamin's case.

# The Playwright & Singer

## Julia Riew

**Education:**
Harvard College, Theater, Dance, Media (TDM) and Music, Class of 2022
John Burroughs School

**GPA and Test Scores:**
GPA, (4.46)
APs, (Spanish (5), English (5), Physics (4), Calculus (5))

**Extracurriculars and Awards:**
Concertmaster of the school orchestra, Assistant Concertmaster for all-state orchestra, Violinist in St. Louis Symphony Youth Orchestra; Starred in high school musical; Captain of the varsity tennis team, four years on varsity tennis team (Two-time State Champions, Metro League Champions); President of Spanish Club and Music Assembly Club; Music director for Arch City Theater Troupe (local theater group); Violin tutor; Founded/Chaired a youth board for a local literacy non-profit called Ready Readers.

Winner, 1st Place, Senior Division, Creating Original Music Project at University of Missouri (2016); Winner, 1st Place, George N. Tuerck Concerto Competition, Philharmonic Society of Belleville (2016); Awarded the Monticello College Foundation Scholarship, Community Music School of Webster University (2015-2016); Composer Semi-Finalist, Chamber Music Student Division, The American Prize, National Competition in Performing Arts (2015); Finalist, American Songwriting Awards Competition for Teen Category (2015, 2016); Winner, 2nd Place, National Young Composers Competition, Community Music School of Webster University (2015); Winner, 2nd

Place, Senior Division, Creating Original Music Project at University of Missouri (2015); Missouri State (MSHAA) Solo and Ensemble Competition Exemplary Honor Rating I for Violin (2014 - 2016); Missouri District (MSHSAA) Solo and Ensemble Competition Exemplary Honor Rating I for Violin (2014 - 2016); Awarded Violin Study Merit Scholarship, Community Music School of Webster University (2013, 2014, 2015, 2016); Winner, Concerto Competition, Community Music School of Webster University (2013); Winner, 1st Place, George N. Tuerck Concerto Competition, Philharmonic Society of Belleville (2013); Winner, Laclede Kids Competition, Ensemble Groups, Piano Trio (2012).

**Hometown:**
St. Louis, Missouri, United States of America

*What are your quirks? What do you think makes you unique?*

I'm always singing something wherever I go and I can't sit still because I always have to be doing something.

*1. What kind of child were you growing up, and what were your interests?*

Since I was such an active child growing up, I never failed to share my interests with those around me. After a few rounds of baking mud cakes and building mulch castles in the elementary school playground, without fail, I would then move onto my favorite game to play—theater. I would cast my friends to act in a play I created and directed and then we would perform it in front of our teachers. At home, I had two older brothers who were very musical and because of their influence, I fell in love with music too and started to write my own songs when I was around nine years old. I haven't stopped since.

*2. How involved were your parents in helping you to prepare for Harvard? How did they help you to learn and grow?*

My parents are my top role models and I wouldn't be where I am today without them. My mom never forced me to try specific activities but instead encouraged me to try as many hobbies as possible to see what I liked, which was how I ended up as a musician and an athlete. At home, my mom loved the fact that her two sons and daughter created a "piano trio," so my home life pulsed with the energy of everyone's passions. I give credit to my mom for making that home environment for us.

When I was growing up, my mom would often volunteer at a literacy program called Ready Readers, so I would willingly go with her to play the violin for the kids and then read to them afterwards, which is how I started the Junior board for Ready Readers. In terms of preparation for my Harvard application, my parents were my top supporters. Since my dad was a surgeon, he was not home most of the daytime, but in the evenings, he was always there to pass on his words of wisdom for the day and encourage us to pursue what we love doing. I remember my mom sitting by me while I practiced violin, eagerly helping me when I fumbled. This helped me build the discipline and habits that I use even today. She was also there every step of the way when I was strategizing my high school and college applications since she wanted to provide as much help as possible. I would hear her call my name from downstairs, reminding me that she was just a floor below if I ever needed help. I really feel incredibly lucky that my parents never forced me to do anything and only encouraged me to trust myself and my pursuits.

*3. What is your most memorable memory in preparation for Harvard, and what was something you experienced that you never thought you ever would?*

The summer before I went to Harvard, I went to Korea for the first time since I was seven years old through the Ewha Summer Program. There I met up with a lot of newly admitted Harvard students, and I remember during one of those meetups, everyone was sharing their majors. It was my turn, and I proudly said that I was going to study music and theater. Then somebody in the group asked, "What are you going to do with that?" Not in a mean kind of way, but in a straightforward manner as most of the people at the meetup said things like biology, computer science, physics—all STEM subjects. I was really taken aback, not by him, but I never really stopped to think that people would question me for my passions or that I had to legitimize them in some way. I had a moment of doubt. *Am I weird? Will I be useless?* When the meeting ended, this thought lingered with me for the rest of the summer.

*4.Study tips you have for younger students.*

Always be ahead of schedule. Tackle the shortest and easiest tasks first, then tackle the hard ones so that you have a sense of accomplishment from the start. For any assignment, I try to start at least one week ahead of time not to procrastinate. Also, I remember back in high school, I gave up on things too early when I really shouldn't have. When I wasn't getting a particular topic, I just remember thinking about why it wasn't getting through my head. Everyone else seemed to get it. But I really should have been more patient with myself.

*5. What do you believe was your "X" factor to gain admission to Harvard?*

In my application, I think it really showed that I was passionate about the arts. When I was in high school, especially in Missouri, where I lived, there weren't many Asian kids interested in theater or music composition. But I started pursuing my interests at a really young age and just kept at them. When I was nine, I began to compose music. When I turned 12, I started songwriting. In high school, I entered a lot of music composition contests and won awards, even for pop songwriting. By the end of high school, I had written over 50 songs and recorded CDs too. For my high school's student theater showcase, I wrote, composed, and directed a full-length original musical. On my application itself, I checked off my concentration interest as Theater, Dance, and Media and expressed my dream of becoming a musical theater writer for Broadway. Overall, I believe Harvard really looks for students who are leaders. So I would say to get into any great school really, the first thing is to find your passion areas and then figure out how to be a leader doing what you love to do.

*6. What are some of the challenges you have faced in school?*

I entered my freshman year as a theater major, but there were so few Asians in my cohort and not to mention, when I wrote my first show, not a single person who looked like me auditioned. The doubts came back and maybe because I wanted to fit in, I switched into Pre-Med by the end of my first semester of freshman year. Looking back, it seemed a bit extreme after all the years of dedication to music and theater. While taking all these science courses, I knew I was lying to myself. Theater was always something that I needed to do, even though my head told me to be "rational" and pursue a "steady" major. The summer before my sophomore year, I became really close with Chloe, the other Asian girl in theater, and we created the Asian Student Arts Project along with our other friend Eric. The first project that came out of this organization changed my course again. I took part in writing a musical called "The East Side," a story about a boy named Ryan who has a crush on a girl in the Upper West Side, filled with themes of cultural identity and gentrification. I think it was important to create a story where I could see myself as part of the narrative. We sold out all five productions of "The East Side," and I kept on getting messages from both Asian and non-Asian students on social media saying how much my play resonated with them and saw themselves in my characters.

Shortly after, I even received a commission from the American Repertory Theater to write a musical for them. After that, I dropped Pre-Med and picked up my theater concentration again. I never thought that I would be the person to actually convince myself that my passions were not as good or beneficial as those of others. Seeing how my creative work was touching people and getting positive reactions, I know now that you can make positive changes with something you really love to do regardless of what anybody says.

*7. What do you find most valuable about your Harvard education?*

The number one thing is the people I've met there. Every class and every social event I attended, I met so many amazing people with passions and talents that seemed unfathomable. Just the rich cultural diversity of these students was something I really appreciated because you learn a lot from each other. This includes the professors at Harvard. They are the top experts in the field and their subjects, and all of them are willing to help you as much as possible. When I went to office hours, sometimes I would end up chatting with them for over an hour about class and everyday matters. The continued support of my family, my friends at the College and my professors have truly made my Harvard experience incredible so far.

*8. What are you currently doing now or plan on doing in the future?*

Since the pandemic, I've been working from home until my senior year starts. As a side gig, I'm doing freelance work for a college admissions company, and during my "work" hours I'm tackling my senior thesis. I'm writing a pop-rock musical adaptation of a play that my friend wrote called, "In the Beginning," which is the re-telling of the story of Eve and Pandora and its surrounding themes. You can find this project and my past theater work on my website juiliariew.com. My ultimate dream is to one day write a musical for Broadway while living in New York or New Jersey and start my own family.

*Summary of Key Points:*

1. For Students: Don't compare your interests with others or think what you are pursuing is useless and unworthy. It is worth it because you care about it.
2. For Parents: Trust and encourage their children's passions and interests.
3. Find your passion areas first and then figure out how you can be a leader while doing what you love to do.

*Review:*

Julia was brave to dive into an entirely different field after having doubts on whether or not her interest would contribute to society. She was even braver to ultimately decide in the end that her love for theater could touch the lives of many in her community. It's okay to leave the path you carved for yourself and it takes courage to admit that what you thought was a sure move to success was the wrong choice for you after all. Julia has shown that it's never too late to start over to do what you love doing.

# The Linguist & Fencer

## Carmen Enrique

**Education:**
Harvard College, BA. Linguistics, Class of 2021
Cambridge Rindge and Latin School

**Extracurriculars and Awards:**
Rowing, Fencing, Latin Club, National Honors Society

**Hometown:**
Palma de Mallorca, Spain.

I spent my childhood in Spain and attended high school in the US.

*What are your quirks? What do you think makes you unique?*

Growing up in a multicultural family (my dad is Spanish, and my mom is Korean American), I have an open view of the world and it's pretty difficult to surprise me. I always want to try new things and travel to new places (the Canary Islands off the coast of Spain, near Africa, is one of my favorite places I've been to. Its volcanic islands are a natural gem). I also love talking to people and keeping an open mind and not taking things too seriously.

*1. What kind of child were you growing up, and what were your interests?*

I grew up in Spain as a ferocious reader. When my mom would go to the U.S., she would bring back suitcases full of English books. I'd bring a book with me to school and have it on my desk so that when the teacher left the room, or we had some time between classes, the first thing I'd do was pick up my book and keep reading. If I was reading a really good book, I wouldn't be able to put it down until I was at the end. I'd spend so much time reading; I would read all afternoon after getting home from school and finish a book every few days.

I was also a very curious child, hoping to learn about everything from imaginary worlds to current events. I was always curious about what was going on in the world, like outside of my own home. It helped that my parents would read the newspaper and tell me highlights and allow me to read over their shoulders and ask questions. My parents wouldn't try to hide or sugarcoat anything, even on heavy or difficult topics such as the refugee crisis or wars.

*2. How involved were your parents in helping you to prepare for Harvard? How did they help you to learn and grow?*

My parents have always provided me with an environment full of stimuli, with many books and engaging conversations about world affairs. They did this because they have always treated me as an adult and shared their interests with me, not because they thought it might get me into Harvard necessarily. When I was in high school, I started developing a deep interest in humanities. I realized that if I wanted to study my passions at a high level with really good professors at a school with well-funded and well-functioning departments, I'd better get into an elite institution. So, the desire to attend Harvard came from me. Neither of my parents knew much about the college admissions process and trusted me in the process. They trusted me to just do it on my own. And I was very deliberate in my approach.

I applied early to Harvard, which became my main focus so I could get in and not have to worry about it for the rest of the year. My parents still wanted to help, of course. They helped me brainstorm ideas for my personal essay, which was very helpful, but I think ultimately you do not want your parents to get too involved. Applying to colleges is stressful enough, and if your parents are also your SAT tutor, essay coach, and college counselor, the home environment could turn toxic. Students need a safe place to come home to and vent after a long, difficult day. You have to be the one who's motivated to get into a specific school. Looking back, I'm grateful my parents never pushed me to a particular definition of success or achievement. They treated me with trust and respect and allowed me to be successful in my own terms.

*3. Study tips you have for younger students.*

My whole life I've been drilled by this idea of time management being critical. But most of us don't even know what that means, and managing my time with carefully planned agendas in different color markers is not something I've ever done. People will tell you to start things early on, but I've always needed a concrete deadline to get started. It took a while for me to realize that I didn't have to be organized in the "color markers" sense or have all plans set in advance to feel and be successful and high achieving. Whatever works for you is good enough. When you have a project or task in front of you, the important thing is to get something done well. It's okay if it takes longer than you expected, or you need periodic breaks, or you need to find inspiration and come back to it. When working on my Harvard application, I dedicated a lot of time to it and found the whole college application process to be pretty stressful. I would get home from school and work on different parts of my application. I spent so much time reviewing it over and over again, going over every single little detail of the Common App that it almost felt like I would not finish. So even if it takes multiple attempts and time to look it over, make sure you are not too hard on yourself.

*4. What do you believe was your "X" factor to gain admission to Harvard?*

I have always loved reading, writing, and learning languages, so I knew I wanted to study something like classics or linguistics, both of which are unpopular majors because people say it may be "useless" or "obscure." Even at Harvard, most of the students have never heard of them. But behind those hallowed gates, you'll find incredible faculty and departments devoted to Ancient History, Hebrew, or 17th Century French Philosophy. Harvard looks to fill its seats with a diverse set of students, not only students who'll end up in Goldman Sachs or become the next president of the United States. As for my "X" factor, I studied Latin in high school and got good grades and received a good recommendation letter from my Latin teacher. I think that Harvard saw that I had an academic passion for a less studied field and that I had the potential to do well in it.

*5. What are some of the challenges you have faced in school?*

Something unique to Harvard is this thing called "shopping week," where in the first week of the new semester you drop into any class for a preview of what's to come before finalizing your decisions. There are so many classes to choose from—Japanese cinema to quantum mechanics—just everything you can imagine. I think "FOMO" is the right term here (fear of missing out), and I ended up putting a lot of pressure on myself to make the right decision in the first go. Despite the amount of flexibility Harvard offers in terms of course selection and major requirements, I noticed myself not fully engaged nor benefiting from this system. I'll continue my studies online (from Spain) due to the pandemic, but I can already see that there will be greater challenges ahead.

*6. What do you find most valuable about your Harvard education?*

When I got my acceptance letter to Harvard, my mom was very excited for me, but my dad was even more excited when he saw the financial aid letters. My parents were very open with me about money and very real about the cost of an American college education. Taking out loans for a college education is foreign from a European standpoint, and I knew I'd need to rely on financial aid. Many students don't realize that these elite schools are one of the most well-funded and often provide the most financial aid and scholarship opportunities for students from low-income and middle-class families. In terms of non-monetary value, my Harvard degree provided me opportunities I would never have dreamed of. Aside from the amazing faculty and range of classes, Harvard provides incredible travel scholarships and various grants. I've received full funding to spend three weeks in Mexico and the Dominican Republic for research projects and various internships. I was about to do a fully funded internship in Brazil this spring break, which turned remote due to the pandemic. Ecuador was also on my schedule. What's even better is that these Harvard professors are so well-connected that they have colleagues all over the world they collaborate with for papers or know each other through conferences. So, if you want to research with a professor in a given country, they can provide you with a list of resources to help you. The international outlook Harvard offers is incomparable to that of most other universities.

*7. What are you currently doing now or plan on doing in the future?*

Right now, I'm pursuing a virtual internship. I was supposed to do an internship in Brazil in person, and while I'm a bit disappointed since this would have been my first time in South America, I still get to practice Portuguese and connect with the locals there. On the flip side, one thing I realized as a result of the pandemic is that traveling is actually really bad for the environment. And obviously you need to travel, and people need to get to places, but amidst all the canceled trips, I realized many of my trips weren't really considered "essential." The pandemic has helped us understand and piece out what is essential vs. non-essential. There's definitely value in being able to appreciate your hometown and being happy with where you are and not always be thinking about the next trip, the next internship, or the next big thing. Instead, I've learned to appreciate the immediate things like family or coming back to your roots.

*Summary of Key Points:*

1. For Students: Pursue the "unpopular" major if you genuinely feel as if it is your calling, despite what others may think.
2. For Parents: Be aware of current events around the world. Parents, engage your children in conversations surrounding these current events.
3. Help can be given in many different ways and by different people, but ultimately, the student has to be the most motivated to achieve his/her goal.

*Review:*

Carmen was very down to earth, someone who was rooted in her hometown but possessed a worldly outlook. Having been raised in a home that was a blend of the American, Asian, and European culture, Carmen radiated sophistication and maturity not often found in her peers. For any topic, Carmen analyzes it from three different (cultural) perspectives, a habit she had formulated as a natural extension of her home life.

# The Tech Consultant & Musical Artist

## Changseob Lim

**Education:**
Harvard College, Computer Science, Class of 2019
Tappan Zee High School

**GPA and Test Scores:**
GPA, (102/100)
SAT I, (2240 (Math: 800, Reading: 730, Writing: 710))
SAT II, (Chemistry (800), Physics (790), Math I (800), Math II (800))
ACT, (34 (Math (36), Science (36), English (320), Reading (32))
APs, (Chemistry, Physics B, Calculus AB, Calculus BC, Microeconomics, CompSci A, Art History, US History, World History)

**Extracurriculars and Awards:**
Founding member & President of Programming Club, All-state saxophonist, Award-nominated actor in school musicals, freelance guitarist, Captain of the math team, President of a pep band, Vice President of Math Honor Society, member of Model UN, member of Science Olympiad, member of Varsity swim team

**Hometown:**
Orangeburg, Upstate New York

I was born in Seoul and lived there until I was ten then moved to China and stayed there for a couple of years. Then, I moved to the States for my middle and high school years. In addition to Orangeburg, I would also call Boston or Seoul my hometown depending on the context.

*1. What kind of child were you growing up and what were your interests?*

I was musically gifted as a child and won many local singing and piano competitions. Looking back, however, I think I enjoyed these activities as a young kid because I just happened to be good at it, not because I felt an inherent gravity towards the arts. I didn't quite find the passion for music until middle school when I obsessed over the Beatles and in turn, slowly learned to play various "rock band" instruments. Later in high school, I read up on music theory, tried my hand at composing, and performed live with many different people in the styles ranging from metal to classical, to jazz.

But I think around the 2008 global market crash is exactly when I moved to the United States. Two years before the crash, I moved to China mainly in part because of the economy and my dad's work had us moving from Korea to China. So, there was a lot of instability going on. I think not just within the world, but also within a microcosm kind of way with my family. I started getting scolded a lot and I started developing a kind of a rebellious streak. Maybe as a response to my parents being angsty and in response to the world around me, but since then, I have been very rebellious. So, in China, it was just a lot of hanging out with friends and it was starting middle school after we got settled in the United States that I started to build my interests such as tinkering with electronics and playing a lot of music. Since middle school, I've been interested in computers in general, whether that be hardware or software. During that same time, I also started playing the saxophone and the guitar. These passions ultimately kind of lead me to where I am right now.

Another interesting memory from my childhood is that I was involved in theater at one point in time. To help me fit in with my friends in middle school and with U.S. culture in general, I was urged by my best friend and my ESL teacher to audition for the theater. Back then, my English wasn't that great but I auditioned anyway, and the panel was impressed with my singing so I ended up getting the lead role in the middle school show. I think it was really funny, as I imagine for the audience too because here was this kid who just memorized his lines without really knowing the meaning of them and singing with a terrible

English accent. But in the end, it was such a great experience for me and I made incredible friends this way.

*2. How involved were your parents in helping you to prepare for Harvard? How did they help you to learn and grow?*

My parents had a very traditional view of college admissions. I, on the other hand, despised studying and anything to do with studying. Starting from middle school, there was pressure from my family to perform well in school and on standardized tests. The conflict in our visions on what my future would look like manifested in verbal, and sometimes physical conflicts. Ultimately, the best thing that my parents did for my college preparations was to have some trust in my competency and to let me handle the entire process myself.

Harvard was never the end goal and it was never even really talked about in the household. It was just acknowledged with the overarching mindset that I should attend a reputable college. Even so, I was doing well enough in school and even on standardized tests. There wasn't much push for me to do well. That being said, my parents were very much involved with my studies at least through middle school. Back in Korea, they put me through all the academies, like every other kid. In China, it was a very similar situation. When I was attending middle school in the United States, I think they tried to continue with that same pattern but couldn't because they didn't have the time and money to continue doing that anymore.

So, in the States, I did a lot of self-studying. My mom would get second-hand textbooks and workbooks from the Korean community or the community at large. She would sit down with me at times and go through the books with me.

Like I mentioned before, I was a little rebellious starting from middle school and I didn't want anything to do with academics. So, my parents and I had a lot of conflicts. I started to fake my practice tests and copy the answers, but only half of them to make sure it didn't look like I copied them at all.

Of course, my parents aren't stupid, and they caught on fairly quickly that I was cheating which escalated the conflict even more. But I think around eighth grade or ninth grade, my parents signed me up for the PSAT. I started coming back with very good results, not only for my age, but just very good results in general and I think that was the turning point for them. That's when they realized that I could kind of handle things on my own. I could do my activities. I could still be playing video games. I could still hang out with friends, but still, be responsible and set my expectations on what I would achieve on my own. Since then, they have had a completely hands-off approach to my school life and my testing life. I guess I have the PSAT to thank for that.

Looking back, a lot of their frustrations towards me was in part due to the economy and partly because we were a low-income family trying to set roots in a new country. My parents were stressed about their own lives and trying to provide for the family so I think their outlet for all that stress was towards my brother and me trying to make sure we were achieving great things so that we didn't have to go through struggles in the future. I think for a lot of parents out there, no matter what situation they are in, they still want the best for their children.

*3. What is your most memorable memory in preparation for Harvard and what was something you experienced that you never thought you ever would?*

My most memorable memories in preparation for Harvard were two things. The first memorable memory is that my Common App essay was a joke. Not in the sense that it was badly written, but it was just a long funny story. My mom somehow got her hands on it and did not like it very much and tried to get me to change it for a while but I stood by my decision that this was the essay that I would be submitting. The second part of the memory is similar. Harvard has optional essays that students can choose to submit. My mom urged me to write them and I specifically remember reading the small text description underneath the prompt. It said, "If you do not believe that this application fully describes who you are, please include an additional essay." And I said, I think my application describes me perfectly, especially with the essay that I wrote for the Common Application, and I decided not to submit one and lo and behind, I got in.

4. *Study tips you have for younger students.*

Honestly having good friends is the best resource a student can have. Good friends in the sense that they are high achievers, or like they would like to achieve highly with you. Friends that share common interests with yourself that you can build and grow together. I found friends that had interests aligned with mine, whether it was music, computers, and acting. Once I found these individuals, then everything else just fell into place. Maybe I was lucky. It sounds like I was lucky. Maybe I had extraordinarily good friends, but I think after making these friendships and spending a lot of time with them to grow together, I think everything else just followed after.

5. *What do you believe was your "X" factor to gain admission to Harvard?*

All of my passions from the saxophone, to acting, to playing various instruments and performing for local gigs, really translated well in a college interview setting, where I could explain my eclectic application nicely.

During my interview, I weaved everything together saying that I had a lot of close friends that I wanted to try new things with that we all found interesting. This included everything from Model UN to Science Olympiad. By doing so, by involving my friends, my interest in these hobbies and for other fields increased in depth. I did enjoy doing these things but I think ultimately, even when it comes to my top accomplishments, whether it was delving into the intersections of music and computer science, the reason why I was doing a certain activity or passion was because of the people around me.

Another thing I want to mention for my admission to Harvard was the effect it had on my brother. I'm sure he's okay with it now, but I remember he wasn't very happy when I got accepted to Harvard because it meant that there would be greater pressure on him from my parents to achieve that same standard and beyond. So, my acceptance came with a lot of joy from friends and family members but also a bittersweet feeling from the tension between my brother and me during that time.

*6. What are some of the challenges you have faced in school?*

I honestly think I came into Harvard with the wrong mindset. I came into Harvard thinking that everybody else was different for me and that they were all super accomplished. They were all national winners, international math and tech whizzes, and other amazing titles. And every person that I interacted with, I was just in awe of them instead of trying to connect with them on a personal level. That kind of tainted my experience during my freshman year.

It's a difficult thing at times. The people you meet at Harvard will indeed be some of the best people you will meet in your life. They're all super smart, super accomplished, and will be even more accomplished later down the road. It's just that I should have realized that I'm in the same boat. But that's also one of the most valuable things I found about Harvard education, is that I shouldn't be so humble when it comes to what I have done and what I can do as well. I have something to be proud of and to share with my community just like everyone else.

Another hardship was that I couldn't keep doing the extracurriculars that I loved doing in high school. So ultimately, I decided to just pursue music and computer science. Even with this choice, there were difficulties I encountered as well because people who are competing for the same spot as you are. They're super accomplished and they're so talented that you might not have a place in certain organizations. For instance, I didn't get into the acapella groups that I wanted to get into during my freshman year. I didn't get the parts that I wanted in the musicals that I auditioned for during my freshman year. That it's kind of a shock for people who come into Harvard. You come to this great university by succeeding in the things that you've been good at in the past and then you expect to pursue these same interests and passions and realize that there are so many people who are also good at what you do, and even better at times. But even so, if you persevere you might find your place.

*7. What do you find most valuable about your Harvard education?*

I'm sure a lot of people have already said this, but the best thing about it is its liberal arts education and the freedom that it grants you not only in the type of education that you want to receive but also in how you want to manage your time. Because of the flexibility of my curriculum, I was able to do all of my computer science endeavors and courses, but I was also able to do all the music opportunities that I wanted to dip my toes into.

8. *What are you currently doing now or plan on doing in the future?*

So right now I am consulting for a tech consultancy. I am doing technical analysis on codebases that are involved in litigation cases. To explain, some tech companies get sued and they can't announce and analyze their code themselves so they give it to our company and they analyze the code. It's really exciting and interesting for me. I see a lot of interesting problems that arise that I didn't quite expect that I would in the field. As an observation, there's not that much difference between academia and the real world as I had once presumed. I'm still thinking and exploring my options, but I know that I want to go back into academia someday, whether that be pursuing a PhD or pursuing a law degree.

As a closure to the readers, I've had opportunities in the past during college where I would speak to children and young students about how I got into Harvard. I was traveling with my acapella group and a lot of people listened to the college acapella music so that they could ask questions afterward. But I want to tell parents that children can excel, especially in the right environment. And I think I could be an example of that. I also really want to tell everyone, maybe not just the students, but to all working professionals out there that try something and it might work out. It might not. But if you get into something, it'll work out. It will pay off maybe not monetarily, but in other ways, you didn't expect.

*Summary of Key Points*:

1. For Students: Find your group of friends with common interests who will motivate you to achieve great things. Even better if you can accomplish great feats by working together with your friends.
2. For Parents: Despite initial hurdles and struggles, children can excel given that they are in the right environment.

3. For your Common Application essays, there is no cookie-cutter formula to get accepted into a certain university. It is best to write about what you feel passionate about writing and most importantly, what you would enjoy writing about.

*Review:*

Changseob's rebellious streak during his middle school years, in the end, gave him the confidence to try new pursuits from performing on stage in his middle school musical despite the initial language barriers to finding his core group of friends in high school. He may have had many conflicts with his parents in the past, but by showing that he could do well on his own, his parents had faith that he would succeed and became more hands-off from that point onwards. He reminds college students to never underplay their accomplishments by comparing yourself to your peers. You are just as worthy to be at your school like the rest of the student body.

# The Empowered & Bookworm

## Angela Yi

**Education:**
Harvard College, AB Social Studies, Class of 2020
Cypress High School, Class Rank (1/780)

**GPA and Test Scores:**
GPA, (Weighted (4.8/4.0), Unweighted (3.9))
ACT, (35/36)
SAT II, (Math Level 2 (800), Korean (780), U.S. History (780))
APs, (Calculus BC (5), U.S. History (5), Language & Composition (5), Literature & Composition (5), European history (5), Psychology (5), Chemistry (4))

Grades:
9th: English 1 honors (A, A); Algebra 2/Trig honors (A, B); Biology honors (A, A); Art (A, A); Swimming
10th: English 2 honors (A, A); Pre-Calculus honors (A, B); A.P. European History (A, A); A.P. Music Theory (A, A); Swimming
11th: AP Language & Composition (A, A); AP Calculus (A, A); AP US History (A, A); AP Computer Science (A, A); A.P. Chemistry (A, A); Physics honors (A, A); Swimming
12th: AP Literature & Composition (A, A); AP US Government (A, A), AP Statistics (A, A); AP Biology (A, A)

**Extracurriculars and Awards:**
Activities: Lexington Junior High School Speech and Debate (Founder, Head Coach), Supergirls (Founder, CEO), Spilt Arts (intern), Cypress High School Speech & Debate (Debate Captain),

Cypress High School Amnesty International (Founder, President), Cypress High School Habitat for Humanity (Founder, President)

Awards: National Forensics League All-American Academic Award, California Music Teachers Association Certificate of Merit Level 10, Orange County Speech and Debate League 1st Place (Impromptu), Bruschke Invitational 1st Place (Policy Debate)

**Hometown:**
Orange County, California

*What are your quirks? What do you think makes you unique?*

I like to think of myself as someone who wants to carve my own space where I find myself in. Right now, I'm particularly interested in how academics could break ground on the YouTube platform.

1. *What kind of child were you growing up, and what were your interests?*

Bookworm would be that one word to summarize my past and still applicable to this day. I read so much that I think I ruined my vision (I wear glasses). While other kids said their favorite place was the amusement park or the toy store, I always used to proudly say that my favorite place in the world was the library. I would borrow the maximum amount of books a person could take out each day. The genre didn't matter: short stories, non-fiction, novels—I would read just about anything I could get my hands on. If I had to choose, my favorite books were novels set in different periods and cultures. Back in high school, I even tried writing some of my own historical short stories. My mom actually scolded me on multiple occasions because I would bring too many books to the dinner table while everyone was trying to eat. I know many moms have the problem of trying to get their kids to read, but my mom had the complete opposite "problem" of getting me to put down my books, depending on the situation. When I was really small, I loved the *Magic Treehouse* series, and then I discovered a series called *The Royal Diaries,* where each book tells a tale about a famous queen or princess from various cultural backgrounds and time periods. Growing up in the States, I had very little exposure to Korean history, so this series was such a great opportunity to get interested in my own heritage and culture. This habit of reading definitely inspired me to pursue my major in Social Studies and Gender Studies. Which basically means my eyes are glued to books 24/7. If I had to choose my all-time favorite book, it's so hard to say, but I did really enjoy *Pachinko* by Min Jin Lee.

2. *How involved were your parents in helping you to prepare for Harvard? How did they help you to learn and grow?*

I became too familiar with my dad's catchphrase on what he called the margin of excellence. He would always tell me to enjoy high school and work 2% harder than what I expect of my own expectations. So that tiny margin of just 2%, putting in that little extra effort, than the people around you will put you ahead of the pack. His positive reinforcement and belief in me definitely helped cultivate the work ethic that I still have today.

Not only that, but I've been incredibly lucky that I had parents who were deeply interested in my interests and did everything that they could to support me. I had annual tournaments with my team at UC Berkeley, and my dad volunteered to drive our entire team from L.A. to Berkeley, which is like an 8-hour drive with a little traffic. In terms of preparation for Harvard, no one pushed or pressured me to apply to the school. My parents had high expectations, but they knew the limits of my capabilities since I was often the one who would be disappointed if things didn't turn out the way I wanted to. They only encouraged me that I could do better next time. My mom introduced me to an upperclassman of mine, the captain of our school's debate team, who got admitted to Harvard during the time when I was a freshman. When we started conversing, I found so many similarities with her, and she really inspired me, and suddenly, Harvard became the dream school of mine to pursue since she made me believe that if she could get in, then I had a chance too. My parents went above and beyond to help me build a strong support system of resources and mentors in high school so that I could achieve this dream of mine.

*3. What is your most memorable memory in preparation for Harvard, and what was something you experienced that you never thought you ever would?*

The nonprofit organization I created in high school, Super Girls, is something I am really proud of. It's an organization to empower young middle school girls to be assertive, feel empowered, and become leaders in their community. Many studies state that girls, especially in middle school, lose a lot of their assertive nature because of gender expectations in the classroom. So, what we did was create a series of leadership summits for the junior high schools in my area, and we even did a spin-off of this program for elementary school students as well! We had a lot of teamwork building workshops, and it was really fun to see all the kids having a good time and learn from the experience. I always tried to find ways to impact the youth in my community positively.

During my junior year, I was even part of this program where I helped kids around my age who were at juvenile detention centers and volunteered to lead creative writing workshops. It helped me understand how young people are negatively impacted by the prison system, such as the lack of resources and opportunities for them to change positively. I was also captain of my high school's debate team, but I also wanted to do something to impact my community more. My solution was to start my own clubs in school. I saw the list of activities and clubs that were already in existence at my school and tried to see which community and social issues have not been addressed. So that's why I created Habitat for Humanity and Amnesty International because they did not have campus chapters at my school. This was a way for my club members and me to have the creative freedom to create our own projects with the institutional level of support.

*4. Study tips you have for younger students.*

I know everyone has heard this over and over again, but I really do believe in this. For everyone, it's crucial to pursue something you are personally passionate about. I know it's such a general statement, but to know what you are passionate about, you have to be aware of what you are good at with the skill sets you have. After thinking about what skills you have, you have to think about what you find yourself doing a lot or things you are drawn to. For me, it was social activism with a heavy focus on feminist issues and issues that involved students. I felt motivated and inspired to constantly work because running a nonprofit or running clubs takes a lot of work and energy.

So, it's important to find something that you're genuinely interested in so that looking back it didn't seem like work at all. To present yourself and all of your past achievements at its best to others, really think about what your unique story is—your narrative to present to the world. Also, remember that each university has its own set of criteria when admitting students, so the fit had to be right. My sister, who I would say is so much more academically talented than me (she did a lot of math competitions and Olympiads in high school) applied to Stanford and Harvard. Harvard rejected her, but Stanford accepted her, and I would say Stanford is harder to get into. So, it really comes to show that each school is looking for students that align with their values and interests.

*5. What do you believe was your "X" factor to gain admission to Harvard?*

I should have requested to look at my admission file when I had the chance, but I think that the admissions team could see I started a lot of projects that I genuinely loved. I had no "strategy" or agenda whatsoever to get into Harvard, but I just did all that I could to fulfill my role as a student activist. So from Super Girls to talking about how to educate the youth at juvenile detention centers, I think that the admission officers could recognize a passionate and driven individual who could bring something to the table and spread my interests with the rest of the Harvard community. I always give this advice whenever someone asks me how I got into Harvard. You have to ask yourself things like how you can contribute to a school that you really want to attend. What are the qualities and exciting experiences that you have that you can share with others? This approach helped me when organizing my narrative for my application, especially for my admission essay.

*6. What are some of the challenges you have faced in school?*

I would say the number one thing is all the unstructured free time that I had, and I had no idea how to use it at first. In high school, everything is laid out and organized for you in periods, so I had to find a way to make use of every hour. There were times when I completely overburdened myself, and I was pulling all-nighters left and right, and it was taking a toll on my health. Finding that balance of getting work done, socializing, and sneaking in naps here and there was definitely a big challenge for me when I first arrived. Also, in high school, I was a big fish in a small pond, and then suddenly, when I came to college, I became a small fish in a vast ocean. There's a lot of support, but also a lot of competition, and you just have to realize that thousands of your peers will be better at something than you, and what's important is to know that everyone has their strengths and weaknesses. Understand your strengths, understand your weaknesses, and work on yourself.

*7. What do you find most valuable about your Harvard education?*

The diploma. Jokes aside, though, the number one thing is the people you will meet there. I've never met people from such diverse backgrounds before, including the professors. One of my best friends from Harvard is from Cuba, and another is from Japan. Just really, you will make friends from every single continent, just about. I grew up in Orange County, California, which is still really diverse, but you still get roughly people from the same background since there are many suburban towns. But I've never experienced the diversity that I experienced during my time at Harvard. I learned so much from the graduate students there who were all brilliant and eager to strike up conversations with the undergrads. You know, Harvard is just this place with *a lot* of nerds. We're all super nerdy there, but we also like to have a lot of fun. That's something that I miss a lot now that I'm in the working world and living life as an adult.

*8. What are you currently doing now or plan on doing in the future?*

Right now, I'm interning at a children's broadcasting company called ICONIX, which is known for the popular kid's TV show *Pororo*, specifically in the business department. This has been really cool since I've always been interested in any type of strategy work, and in January, I'll be entering a consulting firm. My plan currently is to build a few more years of experience learning about business administration before I branch out and start my own business. I'm still young, and there is still some time to pursue a different career or even go to grad school, but I'm excited about the next few years of my life.

*Summary of Key Points:*

1. For Students: Borrow the maximum amount of books you can from the library. Just read a lot. All the time. Even if your mom scolds you.
2. For Parents: Help your children find ways to positively impact the youth in the community through their passions.
3. Understand your strengths, understand your weaknesses, and work on yourself.

*Review:*

Angela has a great awareness of the power of spreading knowledge to others. She knows that just keeping all the secrets to yourself will not change anybody's situation. Instead, your passions and everything you have learned must be shared with others so that communities can grow and develop over time. She also reminds future applicants to colleges to think about not only what the university could offer you, but what you can provide to the university and your future classmates.

# The Vocalist & Bubble Tea Girl

## Sydney Penny

**Education:**
Harvard College, Comparative Literature and German, Class of 2022
Needham High School

**GPA and Test Scores:**
GPA, (4.8)
SAT I, (1440)
APs, (AP Language and Literature (5))

**Extracurriculars and Awards:**
National Classical Singer competition semi-finalist (top 30 in the country), Fidelity Young Artists Competition (solo at Symphony Hall), NATS Boston Classical Singer competition 1st place
Activities: all-state/national choir, film/theater, founder of a special needs music program

**Hometown:**
Needham, MA

*What are your quirks? What do you think makes you unique?*

I have this superstition about the number eight. If there's a train of items but it doesn't reach the number eight, I feel like it is really bad luck. For instance, if I type out six exclamation points one right after the other, I compulsively have to make it eight exclamation points. I've had it for seven years and I can't get rid of it! Another one of my quirks is that I have to get 70% sweet with less ice and with oolong tea when I order boba. It just has to be that way. 70% sugar. And less ice. Always.

*1. What kind of child were you growing up and what were your interests?*

I think the kind of person I was as a child was that I was extremely carefree, loved life, and was very curious about everything around me. I made ordinary things extraordinary by trying to see the positive and fun aspects in different situations and over the years, which translated into how I approached my work in school and my passions. I even remember when I was three-years-old when my siblings were at school, I would have serious and lively conversations with squirrels outside our house. Just for fun and to pass the time. Growing up, I was never pushed in a certain direction by my family, but instead, my parents observed what I naturally gravitated towards and encouraged those interests of mine wholeheartedly. For me, that was singing and music. No one in my family is a professional musician or singer—My dad went to MIT so he is very technical—and I remember my parents once told me the story of when I was three-years-old, and I had just heard a melody of a song on the radio, and I ran over to the piano and flunked out the melody on my own...without any former piano training at all. I know it sounds unbelievable, but it makes so much sense because I would come to know I have perfect pitch later on.

*2. How involved were your parents in helping you to prepare for Harvard? How did they help you to learn and grow?*

My backyard was Harvard. My family would often have picnics at Harvard Square by the design center. I was never made to believe that I had to go to Harvard one day, but because it was something that I saw every day, I was always in my mind whether I was thinking about it or not. When I was about twelve or thirteen, the topic of going to college came up and my parents were never helicopter parents, asking me if I wrote 5000 words on my English essay or if I did this or that. They know this nitpicking really stresses me out so what they did instead was to provide support for my academics, such as finding the right tutors or how my essays were going and if I needed any help. When I was applying to Harvard, my mom would always let me know that she would be downstairs if I needed help proofreading my application essays or needed advice. Not to mention, since I was harsh on myself academically to do well in school, my parents never had to push me or sit me down to make sure I was succeeding in school.

*3. What is your most memorable memory in preparation for Harvard, and what was something you experienced that you never thought you ever would?*

When I knew I wanted to apply to Harvard, I wanted to make sure it was the right place for me in terms of my interests. I wanted to continue singing but was unsure if Harvard would be the best place to do that. So I looked up opera singers that graduated from Harvard, and so many famous names came up that I knew and one of the singers I knew was Liv Redpath, who sings at LA Opera and the MET. So I ultimately took a chance and just messaged her on Facebook, writing something like, "Hello! I'm a junior in high school, and I'm hoping to talk to you about your Harvard experience as a singer!" I was not expecting a response at all, but she responded a few days later, saying to ask her anything. It shows that if you really want something, you will find someone who is inspiring and willing to help you. If they can help you with your goal in any way, it's so worth it just to ask them.

*4. Study tips you have for younger students.*

These are quite practical tips for any student, really. The first thing is to set timers—this was a huge deal for me in high school. I would do this because I have such a small attention span. I would set a timer to 40 minutes and then have a 20-minute break and repeat that repeatedly until I finally "got" the material I was trying to study. The second most important tip I will give you is to have delicious snacks nearby at all times. For me, it was cut up fruit, cheese and crackers, and any relaxing tea. You're burning so much energy trying to absorb concepts, numbers, and information that having your favorite snack nearby will fulfill you. Looking back, I wish I wasn't so hard on myself on subjects I was not naturally good at. Math was that subject for me, and I used to stay one or two hours after school with my math teacher until I understood it because I was blaming myself that I was not picking it up as fast as my other classmates. Instead of thinking what my strengths were, for a while, I was just harsh on myself with the subjects I just needed more time with.

*5. What do you believe was your "X" factor to gain an admission to Harvard?*

In high school, I was competing a lot in opera/classical voice competitions and was succeeding on a regional and national level. I was also acting professionally in theater and film, sometimes taking time off and getting picked up early from school to do so, but still managing to do well in school. But how I applied and extended these interests is how I got into Harvard, I believe. I have an autistic brother, so he rarely got to see me sing on stage or at competitions, which always made me sad. My school had a special needs program, so I tried to make the arts more accessible for people with special needs such as my brother. So in my interview, I talked about how I was able to achieve arts accessibility, and to my interviewer, that seemed unique because I was taking something personal and acting on it. I didn't try to do any Math Olympiad competitions or typical "star student" activities, but just focused on what I cared about and creating an impact in my community through my passions.

*6. What are some of the challenges you have faced in school?*

When I first arrived at Harvard, there were so many. The big ones for me were comparison and insecurity. I was thrown into a group where everyone was valedictorian of their high school. Not only that, I started to compare myself again to the other students pursuing STEM subjects, even though I was clearly humanities. Right now, in my friend group, there are six of us, and five of them are pre-meds, engineers, computer science geniuses. It was tough being the only humanities person in the group and trying to keep up with all the concepts, terms, and ideas they were discussing all the time. They would all be taking this one tough math class, and I would be on the other side writing papers. It's just a different kind of work, but I still questioned myself if I was less smart as my friends were. Just because I was not STEM. But I have come to realize that I'm just on a different path than everybody else.

*7.What do you find most valuable about your Harvard education?*

It is definitely the diversity in what I am learning at school. I was going to either go to Harvard or this music conservatory in London, where I would be on a full music track for performance. I'm so happy I chose Harvard because the breadth of topics I get to learn about is just amazing. So in one semester, I would be taking a class in astronomy, then head over to my Japanese class, then end the day with my animation in film class. I think this ties back to how I was as a child. I just loved learning about everything, and I'm still that same kid in a sense.

*8.What are you currently doing now or plan on doing in the future?*

Right now, due to the pandemic, I am home but doing a remote internship for this German Institute in Vienna, Austria. So I am working with the founder to help him with business models, outreach, and find different target audiences. He likes having my input since I'm a college student studying German. In addition to the internship, I've been writing a lot of songs, making some recordings of them, and submitting them to auditions remotely. One of them was successful, and I'll be performing next weekend at the Tanglewood Institute in Massachusetts, so I've been practicing for that. After I graduate from Harvard, I plan to go to a conservatory in Europe for my graduate degree in opera performance. If I am going to pursue something in the arts, like writing opera in German, since I have a huge passion for languages, then I'd love to be working at a German opera house in a perfect world.

*Summary of Key Points:*

1. For Students: Make ordinary things extraordinary by trying to see the positive and fun aspects in different situations and translate that approach in school, work, and your passions.
2. For Parents: Help your child focus on what he or she cares about and how to create an impact in the community through passion projects.
3. It shows that if you really want something, you will find someone who is inspiring and willing to help you. If they can help you with your goal in any way, it's worth it to just ask them.

*Review:*

Sydney was able to acknowledge her weaknesses. Although during high school and the early years of college, she struggled to stop comparing herself to others, in the end, she was able to trust her passions and legitimize them as her own.

# The Competitive Philosopher & Ultimate Frisbee Player

## Adam Park

**Education:**
Harvard College, AB Philosophy, Class of 2022
Bethesda-Chevy Chase High School

**GPA and Test Scores:**
GPA, (4.0)
SAT I, (1580)
SAT II, (U.S. History (790), Math 2 (800))
APs, (Physics C Mechanics (5), Physics C E&M (5), BC Calculus (5), U.S. History (5), U.S. Government (5), World History (5), Literature (5), Language (5), Microeconomics (5), Macroeconomics (5), Biology (5), Chemistry (5))

**Extracurriculars and Awards:**
Ultimate frisbee, science bowl, Physics Olympics
National AP Scholar, National Merit Scholarship Finalist (received a scholarship)

**Hometown:**
Bethesda, Maryland

*What are your quirks? What do you think makes you unique?*

I do this a lot with friends, but sometimes I like to play dumb even though I know what they are talking about, just to surprise them later. When I have free time, I'm usually playing frisbee with friends.

*1. What kind of child were you growing up, and what were your interests?*

I was a competitive kid growing up, especially when it came to learning. I always wanted to read books that were grade levels above mine. In elementary school, I would use words that I didn't know the full meaning of because I thought it was an intelligence marker. For example, in first grade, I remember instead of saying technically, I would say technologically, because at that time it sounded more intelligent and profound. Back then, I remember I felt offended whenever I was treated like a kid—even though I was a kid.

When I was in the second grade, I wrote a really long email to my school administrator complaining about the school publication, "Time for Kids" we were receiving in the mail had numerous errors and typos in every edition. Yea, I was that kid. I would say I get my competitive nature from my entire family. My mom and dad are lawyers, and I first thought about going to Harvard in elementary school since my mom went there. I was also really into collecting things—rocks, bugs, coins. Just whatever was interesting to me during that time. I was an outdoorsy kid as well and played with the bugs that I found in my neighborhood.

*2. How involved were your parents in helping you to prepare for Harvard? How did they help you to learn and grow?*

My parents were my motivators and role models in my learning. They challenged me with books that were meant for kids a lot older than I was. My mom once offered me $100—which was a lot of money for a little elementary school kid—if I could finish the unabridged works of Mark Twain. I never did. But I did finish a lot of other books that they recommended to me. I even read most of the books that my mom read for her book club. Since she was also a public defender, I helped her prepare for her oral arguments and learned about a lot of cases from her. I was also encouraged to try new things and challenge myself. My parents would recommend this camp or this program to said to check it out but did not force me to do anything. My parents always said to hold academic success in the highest regard, but because they trusted me to carry out this belief, they never really checked my research papers, homework or made sure I had crossed off all the bullet points on my to-do-list. You can say that being competitive and driven was built into my system since my parents are exactly the same way. Yet, sometimes my mom jokes and insists that I would never have found out my passions if she hadn't pushed or guided me in a particular direction. That's something I realized in college. It's a lot harder to do work if there isn't someone guiding and mentoring you in a certain way, but all of my friends and classmates have filled that role. We just naturally motivate each other to do well.

*3. What is your most memorable memory in preparation for Harvard, and what was something you experienced that you never thought you ever would?*

I was a part of an international camp called CISV. It was a really small camp, but it was a volunteer experience I wrote about heavily in my essays because it changed my perspective and helped me to become more empathetic. I first started attending when I was 11-years-old and went once every three years to the international faction and participated in the local program once a year. One year, I was elected to the regional junior board to organize the camp and came across some challenges. Not with the logistics, but meeting people who had completely different worldviews than I did. I grew up in the States, so I was not completely aware of world events at that time. I remember meeting kids from Egypt, and they were all really excited because Arab Spring had just happened, and things were looking up. But then, later, things didn't turn out so well for Egypt. Their reaction was something I thought about going forwards, someone's cultural ties, and the significance and meaning of traditions. When I was 15 or 16, I found myself back at the camp, and there was a huge debate going on about the Israeli Palestinian conflict. A girl was crying, and back then, I didn't understand why. But I realized that it is one thing to just talk about these events and another if you are personally experiencing them.

*4. Study tips you have for younger students.*

In terms of standardized testing, my advice is to do as many as you can. You really have to familiarize yourself with the format and the types of questions they will ask you.

My second piece of advice is to read as many books as you can. If your parents allow it, read the paper while you eat. These days, there are so many kids who are tech whizzes, genius programmers, and future financial analysts. But I think many kids lack the soft behavioral skills that will, in the future, enable them to work with and manage people with these technical skills. For me growing up, I loved fantasy books, especially the ones that came in a series. I can remember some that I was really into—the Warriors series about tribes of cats, the Ranger's Apprentice series, all the Harry Potter books, the Ender's Game series. When I was really little, the Magic Treehouse and the Alchemist series. Both of my parents are huge readers. They would often slide books under my door and let me know it was worth going through. Back then, a lot of my friends didn't understand when I told them I couldn't hang out with them because I was really into this book I was reading.

*5. What do you believe was your "X" factor to gain admission to Harvard?*

There were a couple of things.

First, the fact that I had a privileged childhood and that both of my parents were well-educated. I came from a challenging admission region/demographic as an Asian male from the Washington D.C. area. So, the fact that I went to public school was probably a factor in my admissions. Also, in an interesting turn of events, my interviewer for Harvard happened to be the national president of the organization I had done most of my volunteer work for in middle school. My application showed that I wasn't just a STEM student with nearly perfect SAT scores, GPA, and A.P.s. A lot of kids have this. So, my humanities-focused extracurriculars probably stood out to the admissions officers. I also think my application essay helped me get into Harvard. I thought I had written this great essay back then, but looking back now, it was pretty mediocre. It was about a book, which is a pretty classic topic many kids choose to write about, but the point is that I really enjoyed writing about it, and I guess it showed through the writing. So write something you're going to enjoy writing. One of my friends who got into the University of Washington wrote this genius essay, and it was about avocado toast. It was both hilarious and extremely well-written. I think if you try to be too esoteric, that's when it feels forced. In the end, think about a topic that you genuinely feel like you would be happy writing about. If it's not something you would write, don't write it.

Lastly, I want to acknowledge that Harvard admissions is not a meritocratic process, and that I am privileged—if it seems like I had it easy it is because I did.

### 6. *What are some of the challenges/ hardships you have faced in school?*

Freshman year was the toughest for me because I was not taking classes that I enjoyed. I felt like I was just repeating high school all over again. My mentality in high school used to be walk, don't run. But when I got to college,everyone was running. Even if no one tells you "Run!", it's hard not to when you see people sprinting by you.

This was difficult since I thought I had to challenge myself to the maximum to keep up with everybody. I started as an applied math major but felt a lot of defeat while taking my classes. I just pushed myself from the beginning thinking, okay, I'm just going to take the second most challenging freshman at Harvard.

So, I started off with the second most challenging class and dropped it before the midterm. For exams, I would look at the first question, and then the rest of the questions, and felt like I just didn't care as much anymore. Then, during the summer after my freshman year ended, I read Social Studies seminar type books. I read a couple of books that pertained to the class and really enjoyed them and ultimately decided to pursue Philosophy as a major. I recently read Infinite Jest, and I really like how it talks about social issues with philosophical work here and there. I even wrote about the book in my Harvard admissions essay.

It makes sense for me now why I chose this major. I've always been drawn to discussions, debates, and arguments since my parents were both lawyers, and they will never let me win an argument. Never. Even to this day. So, I spent a lot of time in my room stewing on how I could present a counterargument to them. Although it hasn't happened yet, maybe one day, I will win just one argument.

7. *What do you find most valuable about your Harvard education?*

The people I am meeting. A good rule of thumb is to find all the smart and interesting people you can and keep talking to them. As I'm hanging out with my friends, you can't help but feel that everyone you are talking to will be somebody and successful in the future. One of the best conversations I've had was my first day on Harvard campus. I stayed up until 4 in the morning talking with a friend about everything. We made a pact that night that we would be future business partners and would be roommates together. He lived with me for a little bit. I had zero doubt in my mind that this kid would be very successful—and he is already very accomplished. That night I had one of the best conversations I've had with a friend because we just talked nonstop. I even showed him my notebook where I wrote down all of my ideas, and it turned out he had the same notebook on him as well. We were both applied math majors then, and now he's a statistics guy in private equity. We talked a lot about the right things to do because we both believed that capitalism is inevitable. So we talked a lot about building wealth so that we can float. I'm a product of my parents' hard work, and I'm floating still because of them.

8. *What are you currently doing now or plan on doing in the future?*

Right now, I'm working for the Center for Strategic and International Studies, which is a Washington DC-based think tank. Dr. John Park heads the project I'm in for the Harvard Kennedy School's Belfer Center Developer Center, and I'm also concurrently doing a research project for a venture capital firm in California.

And I am part of the Harvard Computer Society incubation program, where I'm working on a startup with my roommate. It's a busy time for me, for sure. In the future, I want to be an entrepreneur and create my own startup. Maybe even become an author one day too. Going to graduate school is another option for me as well. So far, at Harvard, I've met many kids who are smarter than me and well, not as smart as me. I know it sounds cocky, but I want to make the point that going or not going to your dream school is not the end. The smartest kids I know from my high school ended up going to state schools and have multimillion-dollar valued startups right now. It wasn't even that surprising to me because I saw their talent back then.

One of the smartest kids I met at Harvard in particular always went to bed at 10 pm and never went to class. He just read books all day. He told me I would learn a lot more by not going to class. It sounded insane to me back then. Now, he's at Stanford grad school for statistics. It comes to show that you have to know how to find your rhythm and pace for your future success.

*Summary of Key Points:*

1. For Students: Keep a notebook filled with your ideas in hand and with you at all times. You never know who you will run into or when you may need it.
2. For Parents: Remind your children not to make being smart or working hard for your entire personality. Because when that falls away, you'll have nothing.
3. For your college application essays, write something you would genuinely enjoy writing about.

*Review:*

Adam emulated his parents' hard work ethic and love for reading into his lifestyle. He cites his own intrinsic motivation for his success, but he also equally attributes his parents' influence to where he stands today. In college, he went out of his way to meet and talk with as many people as he could because he knew that everyone had an insight and new knowledge to offer.

# The Aspiring Eye Doctor & Poet

## J. Moon

**Education:**
Harvard Medical School, M.D. Candidate, Class of 2021
Harvard College, History and Science and Statistics, Class of 2017

Deerfield Academy

**GPA and Test Scores:**
GPA, (College (3.98))
MCAT, (517)

**Hometown:**
Seoul, South Korea

*What are your quirks? What do you think makes you unique?*

Do you know the online puzzle game 2048? It's really a stupid simple puzzle game, but I play a LOT of it to this day, especially when I have to think of something. I've been playing it for nearly seven years now. It's a form of my own fidgeting at this point.

*1. What kind of child were you growing up, and what were your interests?*

I was a very arts and crafty kind of kid. I've always enjoyed doing things with my hands, so many of my hobbies involved drawing or making something. There was a beadwork trend in Korea when I was little, so I would spend so much time making necklaces and bracelets. My mom first started it, and then I picked it up after her. I spent a lot of time by myself because I was timid and because of this I became a serious reader. I read a lot of series books like the Babysitters Club and The Bailey School Kids. Every night I would just lie in bed and spend hours reading. In high school I loved writing, so I kept a journal and wrote poems in it. Afterwards I would post them on a personal blog just so I could save them for myself. It was meant just for me. I think the shyness never really went away because here I am, in medical school, just morphed into the adult version of my past self.

*2. How involved were your parents in helping you to prepare for Harvard? How did they help you to learn and grow?*

My parents were both professors, so they were always researching and preparing materials for their university classes. They didn't have much time to spend with me, so they had a very hands-off approach to my education. But because both of them were in academia, I learned by example and seeing them study for long hours each day helped me develop my work ethic. They just checked my report card to see if I was doing okay, and that's about as far as I think they were involved. As far as choosing my major, there was never any pressure from my parents that I had to pursue the sciences. It was a subject I naturally gravitated towards although interestingly I was a history major in college, but that was a last-minute switch. I initially attended Seoul International School but my parents supported my decision to attend a boarding school in the U.S. Still, they felt as if I did not fit into the culture of the school. So when my dad was doing his sabbatical in Wisconsin, I went with him. Even though huge protests were going on at that time due to the budget cuts in the education system, my parents still let me apply to Deerfield because it was something I really wanted to do.

*3. What is your most memorable memory in preparation for Harvard, and what was something you experienced that you never thought you ever would?*

The summer after my junior year in college, I did a summer program at MIT called RSI. Basically, it's a six-year residential program where I got paired with a research mentor. In high school, I also really wanted to be involved in research in some way shape or form, so the summer after my sophomore year of high school, I just cold emailed a lot of college professors, not expecting any response since I was just some high school kid. But luckily one of them had faith in me—I have no idea why—and he hired me as a research intern. I even got paid! Granted, it was minimum wage, but still! It was so exciting for me that I was actually going to get paid for something that I would have done for free. So this was the opportunity that was the springboard to my time with RSI. This professor who took a chance on a little high school kid even wrote me a nice letter of recommendation. I never thought I would take on any biology-related research opportunities since I never took it in high school, but it just ended up that way.

*4. Study tips you have for younger students.*

So one thing I did—my mom actually hated this—but when I studied for exams, after I went over everything on my own, I wrote everything on my bedroom window with a whiteboard marker. I didn't have a whiteboard, and I thought that the window was just fine. I did this as a form of review because I had to see it before my eyes. So, it was just summarizing everything I had just learned and regurgitating it. I found it useful but don't do what I did and make your parents upset. Just buy a whiteboard and write all over it to your heart's content. Another tip I have is to find really good mentors who will guide you in your academic interests and help you grow as a person. I had two mentors I still keep in touch with to this day, and I would not have gotten into

Harvard without them. One of them was my math teacher for three years in high school, and the other was my PI (Principal Investigator) back from Wisconsin, who I was researching for as a sophomore in high school. So, find mentors who share your interests because they will be the ones who will support you in your career.

*5. What do you believe was your "X" factor to gain admission to Harvard?*

Like I mentioned in my "tips" on how I would not have gotten into Harvard without my mentors, I believe they were a huge part of how I got into both Harvard College and Harvard Medical School. They both consulted me on which pathways could be right for me and wrote me really strong recommendation letters. The fact that I also had a lot of laboratory research experience in high school definitely helped. When I was applying to medical school, I was really nervous since I had made a last-minute decision towards the end of my undergraduate years to major in history. But looking back, I think this was also a factor of why I was able to stand out in my med school applications. Writing is an important part of any profession and industry, so during my senior year, I had written a lot of papers concerning the history of medicine, which made me a unique candidate.

*6. What are some of the challenges you have faced in school?*

This might sound a bit obnoxious, but I think the higher I go in my education, the harder it is for me to score better on standardized tests. I can honestly say back in high school, I did not study for my A.P. exams or SATs, except the morning of, and I still got decent scores. But for some reason for the MCATs (the Medical College Admission Test), I suddenly became the worst test taker, and I had to sit down for weeks and review the material. I was stressed because I was competing in a smaller pool, and in the end, my MCAT score was…not that great. But yeah, tests are not my thing anymore. It just comes to show that scores aren't everything, just showing how you are passionate about what you want to pursue is more important.

*7. What do you find most valuable about your Harvard education?*

Hands down, the people. Just amongst my peers, the depth of knowledge that everyone had on so many topics just amazed me. Now that I'm in med school, everybody has the same goal in similar fields, so my conversations are a lot less diverse now than they were in college. As an undergraduate, more people challenged and pushed me to think outside the box. So college was an exceptional time for me because everyone was passionate about what they were passionate about. I actually miss that a lot and appreciate the time I had with my classmates even more now.

*8. What are you currently doing now or plan on doing in the future?*

Right now, I'm in between my third and fourth year of med school, and I decided to take a year off in between to do research in Europe. I'm currently in Boston and researching with a retinal imaging lab using A.I. and machine learning. As for the distant future, I really hope I can become an ophthalmologist one day. I have many eye problems myself, so I really feel at home even just sitting at the ophthalmologist's office as a patient. The cool thing about the fields is that it is always at the forefront of technology. Last year, the first A.I. based medical tool got approved for ophthalmology. I'm even considering becoming a military doctor if I end up going back to Korea, but I'll see how it goes!

*Summary of Key Points:*

1. For Students: Scores aren't everything. You can be the best test taker one day and lose all ability forever the next. So focus on how to show that you are passionate about what you are pursuing.
2. For Parents: Help your children find really good mentors who will support them in their education.
3. Write on your windows, write on a whiteboard. Visualize your learning.

*Review:*

Many parents do not have the time and leisure to monitor their child's education, but what J did was pick up on traits that she thought worked well for her parents and emulate them. She learned by example and received support from academic mentors who encouraged her for many years.

# The Inventor & Experimenter

## Annabel Cho

**Education:**
Harvard College, Bioengineering and Computer Science, Class of 2023

**GPA and Test Scores:**
GPA, (4.473/4.000)
ACT, (35/36)
SAT II, (Math II, (790), Chemistry (710))
APs, (Human Geography (5), United States History (4), Chemistry 3, Calculus AB (4), World History (5), Physics (4), English Literature & Composition (4), Calculus BC (5), Calculus AB (5), Biology (5))

**Extracurriculars and Awards:**
Student Government, DECA, Research, Volunteering project (Legacy 2019), Symphony orchestra, debate, science bowl, Science Olympiad, theatre, cross country skiing, cross country running, music performances at coffeehouses.

Top 5 Finalist at DECA International Competition 2019, Emperor Science Award 2018, National AP Scholar 2018, National Merit Commended Scholar 2018, Top 8 Finalist at DECA International Competition 2018, 2nd Place at DECA State Competition 2018, MN Classic Debate Regionals: 1st, 2nd, & 3rd place finishes 2016-2018, Gold Presidential Volunteer Service Award 2016-2019, National Honors Society, French Honors Society, & Minnetonka Honors Society 2017-2019.

**Hometown:**
Excelsior, MN, USA

*What are your quirks? What do you think makes you unique?*

If you ask any of my friends, they will tell you that I love to make puns in conversation every chance that I can get. Otherwise, I routinely bake custard steamed buns to procrastinate my studying, make three cups of coffee a day, and I'm really into bullet journaling!

*1. What kind of child were you growing up, and what were your interests?*

As a kid, I barely spoke and was extremely introverted. I would hide behind my mom whenever strangers would say hi to me. Then, it must have been sometime around elementary school when my mom signed me up for a theater camp, hoping that I could gain a bit of confidence. Boy, it did work because, after that, I talked nonstop. I asked my parents everything about anything, and I went up to my classmates in school I didn't even know that well just to ask how their days were going. I would sing and dance around the house to verbally and physically express my happiness. I did a complete 180° after that camp.

Whenever I wasn't super chatty, I was also really into making things and inventing already invented things. Since Christmas and my birthday are close to each other, my relatives would buy me these science experiment kits to do, and whenever I finished one, I was excited just to show it to my parents that I had completed something and made something work. At one point, I remember one of these kits was building a circuit where you could conduct electricity with water. One day, I made this little fan that I plugged in and put the wires in the sink and proudly showed it to my mom that I had powered the fan. I just thought building these little things was the coolest thing because I was solving problems, even though they were solved in the real world. Back to the inventions, I remember my family members were always reminding each other if we had our keys, wallet, and whatnot, and as a kid, I had this brilliant idea of a post-it note. To make a small sticky paper to put on surfaces with reminder messages. Little did I know that they had been around forever. I did believe back then that I was the first one to have thought about such inventions. Since then, I haven't stopped trying to find solutions to everyday problems. I'm only half-kidding when I say I'm still a little disappointed I wasn't the first to invent the post-it note.

*2. How involved were your parents in helping you to prepare for Harvard? How did they help you to learn and grow?*

I remember during a car drive once when I was little I asked my parents, "Why is the moon following us as we're driving?" To them, there was never a dumb question. As the daughter of a teacher and scientist, they would answer all of my questions in a way that I could understand. I really admired them because if they didn't know the answer, they would take the day to research it themselves before coming back and explaining it to me. They always had time, no matter how busy they were, to fill my world with knowledge. Looking back, they were patient with me as well. I had such scattered interests growing up, and during one year when I randomly decided to join my school's ski team, they didn't question me at all and went ahead and bought me the skis that I needed. When I ran for my school's student government, they willingly helped me design my campaign t-shirts and posters. I wasn't the best test taker during middle and high school or the student who got the best grades. Still, I had the ambition to try as many activities and hobbies as much as possible to find out what my passion was, and my parents supported this ambition of mine one hundred percent.

By the time I reached the later years of high school, I was stressed and anxious whenever I had a big test coming up. I had restless nights, and I often didn't sleep the night before because I had worked myself up to the self-inflicted pressure to do well. The nights before the big exams, my parents would stay at my desk and bedside, trying to ease my anxiety and make my go-to comfort foods. I'm a pretty picky eater, and I don't like trying new dishes, so these dishes became my safety net during the long hours of studying. Then they would stay in my room until I had fallen asleep to make sure I was well-rested before test days. Aside from my parents, my older brother, who is two and a half years older than I am, was my biggest fan and motivator. He believed I could do anything and achieve anything. When I told my parents I wanted to try out for cross country skiing, they were worried that I would be too exhausted and endanger my health since it was an endurance sport. But my brother pitched in and said that I could learn how to develop the strength and endurance to do cross-country. I rarely remember a time when my family cast doubt on me or rejected any passion I wanted to pursue. So, when the time came to apply for schools, I had the confidence to express what I was passionate about because I had years worth of positive support in my household.

*3. What is your most memorable memory in preparation for Harvard, and what was something you experienced that you never thought you ever would?*

I can't believe I actually did this, but technically, my preparation for Harvard started when I was eight years old. One night, I asked my parents what the best school in the world was because I wanted to go there without knowing what it was or where it was. In a heartbeat, they answered Harvard. So, I searched up the Harvard application online, printed it out, pasted it on my wall, and jokingly declared that I could get into this school one day. Of course, when you're that little, you believe you can do anything and feel empowered by your invincibility. To this day, my parents have kept that application that I printed out in 2008 because they thought it was too adorable that an elementary student was already thinking about colleges.

Interestingly, when it came to my junior and senior year of high school, I had the complete opposite emotion of doubting if I was even worthy of applying to such a top school, so getting accepted was a huge surprise for me. Something that I experienced in high school that I never thought I would ever get to do was to travel a lot during school days. I was in this one club called DECA, and it was a business-oriented club where you perform in competitions, and if you do well, you get to go on week-long trips to places like Disney World even when school was in session. I was only able to do this because I had worked out my schedule months ahead and made sure I would complete all my assignments on time the week I would be gone. I saw great value in experiences outside the classroom, and even though it took three times the effort to make sure I wasn't falling behind, it was something that helped me realize that I could manage my time well and grow as a person.

*4. Study tips you have for younger students.*

Before I realized that being perfect academically would not help me in the long run, I used to think that if I didn't get perfect scores on tests, I would never get into a good college. But once I realized that if I put a portion of my energy into focusing on what I loved to do and not put all my eggs in the basket of being the perfect student, it saved me a lot of unnecessary stress. My dad always said that an hour of my time was so much more than an hour of his time because I was in this pivotal moment where I could impact those around me and find the right pathway for myself. I know this is cliché, but the number one thing that I learned is that you really do have to fail—a lot—to learn something about yourself and improve yourself. I remember when all of my friends were preparing for the PSATs, every single one got the national merit, except me. I thought it was the end of the world for me, but it only pushed me to try harder and use that energy to focus on things I was good at or gravitated towards naturally. I accepted that I wasn't the best test taker compared to my friends, but I did accept that I could put in the effort and try to improve myself more positively.

*5. What do you believe was your "X" factor to gain admission to Harvard?*

My Harvard interview, without a doubt. I actually got the chance to look at my admissions file. Harvard allows its students to look at what your interviewer said about you during the interview and see written comments on the application itself. It was funny because most of my comments on my application were not that great at all. *She didn't do any sports all four years of high school. No perfect test scores. No perfect GPA.* The list went on and on. But, the very last comment said that I was the best interviewee he had interviewed in all of his years of interviewing prospective students. That day, my interviewer was an hour late, and there I was anxiously waiting like it was my Judgement Day or something. But once he came and we started talking, it ended up being a really chill conversation. I talked about how outspoken I was about my emotions and thoughts since childhood, and I guess it transferred into a sense of confidence where I was able to express and display myself the best. So how I honestly presented myself during my interview was how I was able to get into Harvard.

*6. What are some of the challenges you have faced in school?*

It was a lot of sorting out my internal feelings once I arrived on campus. I had never been away from home for more than a week, and not having this support system, in the beginning, was really weird for me. I made friends who did become my support system at school. Still, whenever I encountered the slightest difficulty during my first year, like performing poorly on a small quiz, I would immediately jump to the conclusion that I didn't belong at Harvard. I didn't have my family next to me telling me to get a grip, and of course, I belonged at the school. You'll hear a lot of Harvard kids talk about imposter syndrome, where you feel as if everybody around you is way smarter and better at everything. I remember I applied for this position in an extracurricular activity and thought there was no way I would get it next to all these superstars. But I ended up getting the part. What helped me were these small achievements that happened one by one that helped me get over this syndrome. Whatever school you end up going to, you are there because the admission officers, your family, your friends all believe you deserve to be there. But the most important thing is that you have to realize that yourself.

*7. What do you find most valuable about your Harvard education?*

Surprisingly, not the academics, but the people. Sometimes you find yourself stuck in a rut and feel helpless that you can't do anything. But then your roommates come in, or friends stop by to say hello, and they are just so excited about something going on campus or a topic that they learned about, and it's this positive reinforcement that uplifts you and helps you find your motivation again. I've never experienced anything quite like it. Being in an environment where everyone is passionate about their interest and can get other people excited about it. Unlike high school, where everyone compares their test scores, I've never had anybody tell me how they did on their exams, so you definitely do not compare yourself as much to your peers. During my Harvard interview, I remember asking if the Harvard student community is competitive or cooperative because I was worried everybody was going to be cutthroat. But it really isn't. My friends and classmates have been nothing short of supportive in my times of need and have only encouraged me in my pursuits.

*8. What are you currently doing now or plan on doing in the future?*

As of now, I'm planning on going back to school, and I am doing an internship at a biomedical device company called Medtronic. It's a lot of intern work, but just connecting with many different people in the company, talking to them, asking them questions, and learning about their life story have been rewarding for me. Other than that, I'm doing some research work at Massachusetts General Hospital in joint association with Harvard Medical School. I'm just doing a little bit of image data analysis for them. Still I'm thrilled I have this lab opportunity because they're very adamant about making sure that everybody is learning. In the future, I'm not sure yet exactly what kind of pathway I want to be on. I want to do something related to bioengineering, but more on the business side. I don't think I can be a scientist in the lab doing super detailed research. I am probably somebody who wants to do more of the project planning or project management in the industry. I know I definitely want to go to business school at some point. But it's something I'll have to figure out.

*Summary of Key Points*:

1. For Students: You have to fail—a lot—to learn something about yourself and how to improve yourself?
2. For Parents: Indulge their sense of curiosity and encourage your children to ask questions at all times.
3. Have the ambition to try out as many activities as possible to know your passions.

*Review*:

Annabel has been on both sides of the spectrum, where she felt as if she was an utter failure in comparison to her peers to being the most confident individual who is not afraid to speak from the heart. Because of her experience with both sides, she learned from her own mistakes and turned it into her assets. Since she is naturally a very curious person, she embraces both positive and negative events in her life as a learning experience.

# The Historian/Computer Scientist & Violin Virtuoso

## Alyssa Kim

**Education:**
Harvard College, History and Computer Science, Class of 2022
River Dell High School

**GPA and Test Scores:**
GPA, (97%)
SAT I, (1570)
SAT II, (Math 2 (780), Chemistry, (780))

**Extracurriculars and Awards:**
Competitive violin, Model UN, Science Research, Student Council, Volunteer, National Youth Orchestra, Juilliard Pre-College, Debate, Chemistry Olympics, Girls State

**Hometown:**
River Edge, NJ

I grew up in a different town called Wallington in New Jersey. It was not that great of a school system, and it was largely populated by Polish immigrants. So, a lot of my friends growing up were Polish and there weren't many English-speaking families. Then my mom heard about Bergen County's great school systems so we moved to River Edge for my elementary, middle, and high school years.

*What are your quirks? What do you think makes you unique?*

I was always optimistic growing up, even under a stressful high school environment. I always found a way to enjoy and have those moments under control.

*1. What kind of child were you growing up and what were your interests?*

I was a child that loved going to school and tried my best in every subject. I was competitive, but not to the point where it was blatantly obvious. I found that one of my greatest interests was music and I picked up a lot of different instruments and developed confidence knowing that I had the ability to quickly learn how to play all of these instruments compared to my peers. I also didn't watch that much television when I was a kid, so I ended up reading a lot of books and used my time productively.

Personality-wise, I was somewhere in the middle of being outgoing and shy. I think I really thrived in social environments. My personality and most of my interests were centered around music. I eventually focused on playing the violin a lot and that was mostly my main thing throughout middle and high school. But before that I learned a lot of different instruments and really loved it. I realized that I had a talent for playing a variety of instruments.

*2. How involved were your parents in helping you to prepare for Harvard? How did they help you to learn and grow?*

My mom would always encourage me to take the most advanced classes, scheduled lessons and handled the logistics of violin competitions, and kept me accountable for a daily routine. My mother was a stay-at-home mom so she was able to dedicate a lot of time researching resources in the area and reading about how students were able to gain admission at top schools. My mother also learned a lot after going through the college application process with my older brother so she was able to help me a lot more after that first experience. My dad has always been a hard worker to provide financially for the family. He wasn't really hands-on in terms of the activities I was involved in but always made sure I was able to take as many lessons as I needed and provided for any other opportunities I wanted to pursue.

My mom might not have known about the specifics of courses, but she always had recommendations of what I should do if she didn't have the answer. She would suggest I make an appointment with my guidance counselor to talk about course planning and reminded me to take advantage of every opportunity that was presented to me. In terms of shaping my personality, I have always admired the fact that my mom was an independent person. She inspired me to realize that in the end, I have myself to rely on. I can take on suggestions from other people in terms of how I should prepare for college, but I have to find out what I can do myself to prepare my applications for these schools.

*3. What is your most memorable memory in preparation for Harvard and what was something you experienced that you never thought you ever would?*

Something I realized reflecting back was that I had always easily achieved the grades that I wanted without having to put in too much effort. But there was a point where I lost my grip with academics, especially with my math courses. At one point I struggled in my math class not really because of the content but because of a personal conflict I had with a teacher that really impacted my grades. So during my junior year, there was a dip in my GPA and when I looked at my admissions file once I got to Harvard, there were notes inside saying how they noticed I didn't do so well academically during that time and how other things like doing a lot of violin competitions made up for it. They probably made the correlation that my grades suffered briefly because I was constantly travelling for all of these competitions. So that was something I didn't realize affected my application so much, but it did. Thankfully I had an explanation to support the dip in my grades. It was weird because I really had doubted my skills at a certain point. I doubted a lot about my abilities, but I think it was just kind of a bump in the road that I was able to get over quickly.

*4. Study tips you have for younger students.*

Yeah, I think one major piece of advice other than studying is to really connect with not just your teachers, but those who are also writing your letters of recommendation. By having more of a personal relationship with them, they will know what you want to achieve in the future and what kind of person you want to be. You won't just be any student from their chemistry or Spanish class, but they will see you as a future leader with big aspirations to change the world. I learned the importance of this watching my older brother go through high school. I would say he did exceptionally well but I saw that he didn't really have any deep, meaningful relationships with any of his teachers. I think what I took from that was to really work on relationships with people around me.

In terms of preparing for standardized tests, I know a lot of students rely on after school academies and tutors but what really helped me was putting the responsibility on my own shoulders, knowing that I am the only one that can help myself. It is also really important during the time you prepare for college applications and standardized tests, to remain calm as much as possible because everyone else seems to be a ball of stress. Refrain from getting caught up in the anxiety.

*5. What do you believe was your "X" factor to gain an admission to Harvard?*

Aside from dedicating every weekend I had to play music at Julliard's Pre-College Program and winning local and national music competitions, I came from a public high school and area where not many kids were sent to Harvard often so that definitely helped as well. For my applications, I really focused on both of my essays with the core theme of cultural exchange—how I interacted with people not just through music but through language, kindness, and other forms of communication that we don't really call communication in everyday life. My supplemental essay was more analytical about my surroundings and how I see the world in a different perspective and I think they really appreciated how my ideas seemed fresh. They did mention that in my admission files as well.

I think for me, being in love with music was not only about the music itself, but more about the people and culture behind all of the music that I played and the people that I've met. And so originally I wanted to study something along the lines of anthropology, but coming in I just really wanted to explore all different kinds of majors and move away from music. I think I always knew in my heart that I didn't want to have a career in music, but wanted it to have a special place in my heart. So I am very involved with extracurriculars related to music on campus. There is a huge music community here at Harvard.

*6. What are some of the challenges you have faced in school?*

During high school the only hardship I would say was managing my time because most of my weekends were fully dedicated to music. When most people had a weekend to prepare for school or other academic activities, I had to fit those in a lot less time. I also was not able to spend much time socializing or hanging out with friends so it was definitely a challenge to feel like I wasn't enjoying my youth as much as I could have. Once I arrived at Harvard, I wanted to change that so I am really focused not only on developing friendships with my professors, but on spending a lot of time with my friends who are all so incredibly talented and just as inspiring as my professors are. The challenge that I had in high school has turned into a positive thing in my life.

*7. What do you find most valuable about your Harvard education?*

Something that I really value about just being at Harvard is the amount of diverse thought and people that are there. You have so many opportunities at school for you to connect with people not with only similar interests, but very different people as well. I remember some nights my peers and I would talk up until 4 in the morning almost neglecting our assignments for these conversations. I feel like those conversations made me mature in a different way. I think I was always mature in my work and perspective on life but once I got into Harvard and made friends, I reached a whole new level. I also find the pre-professional aspects of all the organizations on campus really helpful. I'm part of finance and computer science groups and seeing how motivated everyone is and how willing people are to share their resources with their peers is something I have never experienced in high school. Back in high school, everyone was competitive and wanted to keep the best resources and secrets to themselves. But knowing that everyone had such a difficult path to get where they are right now, I think collaborating with people has been a lot more fun and honest and genuine at school.

One really interesting random class I ended up taking was about biopolitical animals but in the class, it was only me, another undergrad student, and a grad student—three people in the course. Usually people try to find really small classes for that intimate classroom setting but this was even less than the eight people which is considered the smallest sized course possible. So having three people against one professor really gave me a chance to learn so much more because I was in a course where I had to take up a third of the class in terms of participation. This was a really interesting learning experience where I could just focus on learning, improving my writing, and my critical thinking skills but not necessarily worrying about my grade.

In terms of being labelled as a Harvard person, I haven't had experiences yet where I was treated differently but given advantages just because of my educational background. I think that's helped me stay very humble and make sure that everything I do is a product of my own work and not because I go to a certain university. I feel very lucky to have even gotten in so I don't take it for granted.

*8. What are you currently doing now or plan on doing in the future?*

It's been really hard to plan for this summer especially with everything going on considering a lot of loss in job opportunities, but I'm interning at a venture capital firm right now, which I just coincidentally started during last semester. For now, I think planning for next year's summer as well is important to me. There's a lot of planning that goes on and so I've just been working closely with the academic advisors that are available to me to just have a timeline so that once junior year starts I won't be overwhelmed with the deadlines. I'm even actively considering law and business schools for the future.

*Summary of Key Points:*

1. For Students: Take the initiative and responsibility to look for resources on how to prepare for college and college applications. You may be receiving a lot of help from others, but make sure you know all the details of the process as well.
2. For Parents: Preparing your child for the college application season can be a daunting process, especially if it is your first time. The most important thing is to gather as many resources as possible to make informed decisions.
3. It is best to show improvement over time, but in the case that a student hits a bump in the road and temporarily shows a dip in grades, application reviewers will take into consideration what external factors could have affected a student's performance.

*Review:*

Alyssa dedicated most of her life to music and playing instruments even though she knew that she would not make a career out of it. How her years of dedication to the music world helped her was evident in her applications. She decided to focus her essays on how she communicated with her surroundings through music and language and was inspired by the people and culture behind the music. She also reminds us of the importance of cultivating meaningful relationships with those around us to grow and learn as an individual.

# The Debater & Hair-Length Policy Resister

## Kyle Kim

**Education:**
Harvard College, AB Government, Class of 2019
*Performed 2 years of army service in between.*
Korean Minjok Leadership Academy

**GPA and Test Scores:**
GPA, (4.99/5.00)
SAT I, (2320)
SAT II, (Physics B 800, Math II C 800)

APs, (Macroeconomics (5), Microeconomics (5), Literature (5), Comparative Politics (5), Physics B (5), Calculus BC (5), US History (5))

**Extracurriculars and Awards:**
Student Council Member, Debate Captain, Co-captain of Mock Trial Team, President of a Vocalist Club, National Rep./Champion in Debate competitions.

**Hometown:**
South Korea and Boston, Massachusetts

South Korea is my home country, the place I was born and raised in up until college. However, Boston has been growing on me for the past 6 years, and I now consider the U.S. to be my second home.

*What are your quirks? What do you think makes you unique?*

I am really into engaging in any type of conversation, even one that leads to a healthy debate. Sometimes, I get into trouble because of this. I really like to talk about anything from daily life matters to the wrongdoings of the current administration.

*1.What kind of child were you growing up and what were your interests?*

As a child, I read a lot. I was drawn to Korean biographies and "entry-level" literature, like *Animal Farm*, when I was in middle school. The more I read, the more I placed rationality and reason above anything else. That's how I became a debater—a stubborn one, too. I remember getting into a lot of "arguments" with teachers back in Korea when I tried to resist regulations that I didn't think were reasonable. For example, there were policies that enforced a certain hair length or demanded that students donate money to organizations and causes. Such policies were really just unacceptable to me. For the life of me, I couldn't see any correlation between having my hair cut a certain way and my academic performance. As for the mandatory donations, I thought it completely defeated the purpose of voluntary contributions. You see, I would have happily donated, regardless.

In Korea, there is a pressure to conform. Therefore, as an inquisitive kid who would always speak his mind, my actions of questioning the authorities around me were always frowned upon.

*2. How involved were your parents in helping you to prepare for Harvard? How did they help you to learn and grow?*

I was a curious, stubborn, and analytical child. I would constantly ask questions, seeking clarity on observations I did not understand. "Why is the sky blue?" "Why did the animals in *Animal Farm* end up exactly where they had been before the revolution?" Fortunately, my parents were pretty patient people. My dad, a professor who enjoys teaching, would tirelessly break down difficult concepts in a way I could understand.

Both of my parents were incredibly supportive and helpful throughout my childhood, nudging me to explore my curiosity. They gave me a lot of freedom, and encouraged me to pursue a wide variety of activities so I could identify my personal preferences. At one point, I was trying out 10 to12 different extracurriculars, including tennis, swimming, soccer, and piano, just to find which ones I was passionate about.

At any point, if I didn't want to pursue something, my parents would simply tell me to stop. They never forced anything onto me. I remember complaining to my parents about this one academy that I didn't want to attend anymore. To my surprise, my parents told me, "You don't have to go if you don't want to. We wouldn't want to pay to force you to do something you don't really want to do." They were really understanding of my situation. That's when I realized, "Oh, okay. I'd better think about whether I want to stop going or not." It's kind of scary if you're told at age 13 that you don't have to study anymore or pursue extracurriculars, and can drop out of the conveyor belt. You start seriously thinking about your own decisions and its consequences.

In senior year of high school, my parents invested a considerable amount of time and effort to help me write my application. Over weekends, we would spend hours together brainstorming, editing, and revising application materials. They were both my editors-in-chief. Although the story and contents on the application were about me, crafting the application was most definitely a team effort.

I have my mom to thank for my decision to apply to Harvard. When early action came around, I remember my mom saying, "This is early action, and you'll still have regular decisions left. If you don't reach for the stars now, you're going to regret it for the rest of your life, regardless of whether you get in or not."

*3. Study tips you have for younger students.*

In terms of study tips, I'd say students should plan early and follow through with unflinching focus. Before every exam, I would count down how many days I had left and realistically budget how much time I would need to master the exam content for each subject. Usually, I'd set up a schedule for two to two-and-a-half weeks of prep before midterms and finals. I would then try to follow that schedule to a T, and be really hard on myself if I couldn't follow through. Every student has the potential to excel. It's not intelligence that varies greatly among students or matters to a large extent, but rather, discipline.

I also knew subconsciously that I needed to produce academically stellar results if I wanted to allow myself the luxury of having fun with friends, to speak out in class, and receive the support of my family, teachers, and peers. If my exam grades were to drop, I knew that I would not be able to enjoy hanging out with my friends. In other words, academic achievement was an emblem of self-proof, a certificate or pass required for me to go enjoy the things that I wanted to do the most. But once the exam period was over, I would reward myself by playing computer games for eight or nine hours straight to my heart's content. I've embraced that "work hard play hard" mentality.

I was a humanities kid who enjoyed reading English literature and debating politics. Subjects like math and science, while enjoyable to a certain extent, were not my forte. To do well in those subjects, I'd honestly have to invest double or triple the amount of time some of my peers do. I was painstakingly slow since I had to break down everything, and then walk through every step to understand from the ground up. As a last resort, I'd end up memorizing the content without really understanding the fundamentals. And that is one of the things I really didn't like doing. In the case of one exam in AP Physics class, I memorized every single formula and every single problem set by rote, since I had limited time to understand it all. This is how I got through subjects I either disliked or had a harder time grasping.

*4. What do you believe was your "X" factor to gain an admission to Harvard?*

I was not afraid to show true self. I had faith that the most genuine and raw version of me would also be the most interesting and appealing. If Harvard didn't want me for who I am, then I probably didn't belong there. So, it was more like I was finding a school that's right for me, and not the other way around. Maybe Harvard liked that honesty and confidence.

I also chose to feature debate prominently in my college application, even when teachers and college counselors heavily advised me against it. Debate in college applications was cliché, a red ocean, and frankly not doing very hot in college admissions. A lot of people told me straight-up to quit debate, to do something else, or at least to not make that the main aspect of my application. But upon reflection, debate was what I still liked the most and had defined who I was most aptly. So, I made a bold move to feature it as the front poster of my application. I also submitted a resume that went beyond the traditional bullet points of achievements and stats, but also included descriptions of why I chose to participate in each of the extracurricular activities listed. While you should follow the given formulas and templates, within those boundaries, you can be a little bit creative and showcase your genuine self.

Listing your extracurriculars and awards, no matter how extraordinary they may be, is just 50% of the application process. The other 50% is to really present and frame your accomplishments in a way that demonstrates and maximizes your strengths. A well-crafted story that highlights who you are and what you've done is crucial. What I've seen so far is many students not putting enough effort into that aspect of the application process. They spend two-and-a-half years working towards becoming an Olympian, yet only take two weeks of writing the actual application. It's a huge waste of potential. You want to strategically think about your strengths, and showcase these on paper.

*5. What are some of the challenges you have faced in school?*

This may be a really controversial statement, but I actually think Harvard was less academically challenging for me than high school. I think that only goes to show just how hardworking students are back in Korea.

The most challenging aspect of Harvard was assimilating culturally into the U.S. system. Despite my fluency in English, I was a foreigner in the United States because I've spent my whole life in Korea. As such, engaging with my peers and professors within the U.S. context at Harvard required a bit of extra effort. I had to become more proactive and extroverted by looking for opportunities where I could meet different people, listen to their stories, and continue to push myself out of my comfort zone.

*6. What do you find most valuable about your Harvard education?*

I definitely think Harvard's most valuable assets are the people: my peers. My best memories of Harvard involve late-night discussions with roommates and housemates, even at the expense of studying for finals. Harvard students are generally highly ambitious; they want to change the world and really make a name for themselves. My friends have gone on to work at top banks like Goldman Sachs or at tech companies like Google. Some peers go out to start their own businesses, travel around the world, run nonprofits, or even lobby in Congress. Being surrounded by a crowd like this really inspires me to want to live up to their examples.

Additionally, Harvard bestowed me with the confidence that I can really do anything I set my mind to. Getting into Harvard was probably one of the most challenging accomplishments in my life thus far, and I now have the confidence to overcome any other challenges life throws at me.

*8. What are you currently doing now or plan on doing in the future?*

I am currently working in management consulting, which means I get to experience a lot of different industries. I'm still asking myself what I want to do in the future. I'd like to make a positive impact in the world, whether that be by helping people or companies solve their problems so that they could become a better version of themselves. I also hope to work on projects that genuinely interest me and stimulate my intellect. Ultimately, I want to be happy. I am going to strive to find the right work-life balance, and aim to contribute to others and society in a meaningful way.

*Summary of Key Points:*

1. For Students: If you haven't already, read *Animal Farm* by George Orwell. It will give you the confidence to challenge others, and to stand up for what you believe is right for life.
2. For Parents: Contrary to popular belief, intelligence is not the strongest measure of student academic success. Instead, self-discipline contributes greatly to one's potential to excel. Craft a resume that goes beyond the traditional bullet points of feats and statistics. Be sure to include strong justifications for why you chose to participate in each extracurricular activity you list.
3. You will receive a lot of advice on how to portray yourself for your college applications. Sometimes, staying true to your instincts, such as how Kyle heavily featured his active involvement in debate despite others' objections, is the way to go.

*Review:*

Kyle did not shy away from speaking his mind, and even challenged authority at times. It's no wonder he had a knack for debate. He demonstrated discipline as a student, making sure any task at hand was completed thoroughly, and rewarded himself once he had accomplished a goal. He presents the point that college counselors in high school can be a resource, but, ultimately, students have the freedom to choose how to present themselves in their applications. If Kyle had blindly taken every piece of advice he was offered, instead of going with his gut, then perhaps his chances of getting into top schools would have been different.

# The Bookworm & Harpist

## Danielle Nam

**Education:**
Harvard College, AB Economics, Class of 2023
Mountain View High School, Class of 2019

**GPA and Test Scores:**
GPA, (Weighted 4.7-4.8, Unweighted 4.0)
SAT I, (1560)
SAT II, (Korean (780), Biology M (800), World History, Math 2)
APs, World History (5), English Language and Composition (5), Biology (5), Spanish Language and Culture (5), Calculus BC (5), U.S. History (5), Physics I (5), Statistics (5), Psychology (5), Macroeconomics (5), Government (4), English Literature and Composition (5))

Class Rank, Top 10

**Extracurriculars and Awards:**
Harp (competitions and concerts), volunteering to play the harp for patients at the local hospital, Biology club officer, Speech and Debate (minor engagement).

National Merit Semi-Finalist, National AP Scholar, USA Biology Olympiad Semi-Finalist, placed several times in international harp competitions.

**Hometown:**
Silicon Valley, California

My dad moved to the United States back in 1997 to do his Masters and Ph.D. in electrical engineering at Stanford, and so we've been living in the Bay Area and the Silicon Valley area ever since.

*1. What kind of child were you growing up, and what were your interests?*

I was an imaginative and curious child who spent more time with family than friends. My mom used to tell me that when I was maybe six or nine months old, I was a really active child, and I would hold my shoes up to her to let her know that I wanted to go on a walk. I think I really liked going outside and saying hello to people. My mom and I would make frequent trips to the local libraries for excursions because I was constantly reading. Starting at age three, I spent hours reading every single day. Books were my primary entertainment source as I was only allowed to watch TV on special occasions like whenever we went on family vacations or if I was at a friend's house. My mom would read10 to30 books to me every single day. I remember that, in the back of my elementary school classroom, there were around 300 books on the bookshelf. By the time the school year was over, I had gone through all of them.

*2. How involved were your parents in helping you to prepare for Harvard? How did they help you to learn and grow?*

While both my parents are immigrants to the United States and not that fluent in English (although my dad speaks relatively good English), I am appreciative that my parents made a point about learning languages. They also put in a lot of effort to make sure I had a lot of cultural experiences and excursions such as trips to parks, museums, and fairs nearly every day. They emphasized that learning happens just as much outside the classroom walls as well as inside the classroom.

While my parents gave me extracurricular workbooks during elementary school, I did not have any private tutors, nor did I enroll in SAT boot camps during high school. My parents and I have always been very close, and I would ask (and still do) for their input whenever it came to academic decisions. I also spent so many hours discussing my college application essays with them. I felt that the people who had known me literally since birth would best guide me in communicating an honest and accurate narrative. At the beginning of the school year, we would do brainstorm sessions where we sat down and thought about what I had done. And later, when I was writing iterations of my essays, the essay ideas themselves and the logical structure for the essays were something that I could describe to them and get feedback on.

My parents also supported me in my music career—I was a harpist and frequently traveled for competitions and concerts. By junior year I was doing around four to five different competitions every year. My mom helped with booking flights, hotels, figuring out the logistics— things I would never have been able to handle as a high schooler. My dad also drove me every single week to volunteer at a local hospital. My parents never forced me to do anything I didn't want me to do, but I would never have been able to push myself to achieve to this extent without their support.

*3. What is your most memorable memory in preparation for Harvard, and what was something you experienced that you never thought you ever would?*

Music was a big part of my life before college, although it is not nearly as much now. There was a major harp competition in Hong Kong the fall of my senior year, arguably the most stressful time for high schoolers because it's time for college apps. I had initially applied, not really expecting anything, but I got invited to compete in the live round in Hong Kong.

I remember having to make a difficult decision between something that seemed like a long shot, but that I wanted to do and something that would have been the logical decision—to stay and work on my college apps. Although I had attended several national-level competitions, I had never competed internationally. I knew it was a long shot, but I really wanted to go and see the competition, and, to be perfectly honest, to run away from the pressure of college applications even for a brief moment. In the end, I ended up going with my mom.

We left on a Thursday, after the sixth period at 2 pm from school (yes, I oddly still remember the time too) and went directly to the airport and arrived on Saturday morning in Hong Kong. I went in the afternoon to practice, and even then, had to wait in line for a long time, since I didn't have my harp with me. On Sunday morning, I competed on stage. I ended up getting 2nd place, which I did not expect at all! After attending the award ceremony that Sunday evening, just like that, we flew back just in time for school the next day. As crazy as that experience was, I'm really, *really* glad I did that. For one thing, it's one of those memories that I will cherish having spent with my mom, but also, as I haven't placed at an international competition before, at that point, I definitely think this experience helped me in terms of my college apps. And while I'm down to earth and cynical at times, this experience taught me that sometimes it's okay to take a leap of faith and try things that you don't think are going to work out because, well, they just do.

*4. Study tips you have for younger students.*

Since I had to balance time practicing on my harp and schoolwork, I learned how to manage my time wisely early on. For me, it was better to study alone because I could concentrate better, although I find that group work and study groups are really helpful now in college. In my case, I didn't go out that much during high school either, so that I could focus on music, school, and extracurriculars.

Next, I think taking classes that you are actually interested in is important, which may sound pretty obvious. Still, a lot of people take classes simply because they think it looks good to colleges. And while taking difficult subjects may look good, getting good grades in subjects you like will look even better. It's much more challenging to get good grades if you hate what you are studying. I'm sure some people have the willpower to plow themselves through things regardless, but choosing subjects you are genuinely interested in and do well in helps a lot. As for me, I tried to look for things that I really enjoyed about each class and focused on that to get myself motivated to study when things got difficult. Just know what your passions are and show that on your application. I don't think colleges expect you to be doing everything and doing them well. As long as you have a focus area (maybe you take regular U.S. history but you take advanced biology and volunteer at a local laboratory) and develop T-like expertise—that is what the admissions officers actually look for.

*5. What do you believe was your "X" factor to gain admission to Harvard?*

I've always loved music, and I think my extracurriculars were the most critical factor for me personally. I started playing the harp when I was six. I started piano when I was five, and apparently, I started to record my own singing when I was about two or three years old. As I have previously mentioned, in high school, I competed and placed in international harp competitions, which probably contributed to my standing out. The harp is a unique instrument choice, and I was competing at a pretty high level to a point at which I was considering conservatory schools for college.

I was also involved with public service. I volunteered as a tutor and did voluntary music performances since middle school. I would play in a hospice unit, but this experience went beyond just playing music. Many of my audience members were veterans from the Vietnam War, WWII, and the Korean War who would all share their incredible life stories with me after the performance. I remember I could feel myself maturing and taking on new perspectives because what they went through, the service they did for their country, was unforgettable for me to hear directly from them.

*6. What are some of the challenges you have faced in school?*

I want to talk about a particular dilemma I had even before arriving at Harvard. During the fall of high school senior year, my dad and I went on a four day drive down along the east coast to visit all the schools. At Harvard, I touched the foot of John Harvard for good luck. When I arrived at Princeton, it really stood out to me because it had a calm atmosphere, which I needed at that point in the stressful college application process, so I applied there early decision. I didn't think I would get into the Ivy League school, but I still thought it was worth a shot to apply. I didn't expect to get in, and so when I got in, I was very, *very* surprised.

For Harvard, I applied regular decision. When March came around—prom season—I was about to go try on a dress, and that's when I got the mail telling me I got into Harvard. I had to make a pretty difficult decision between Harvard, Princeton, and Stanford. I made a spreadsheet and listed a bunch of factors like location, weather, classes, friendliness of the student body. I was intimidated by Princeton's grade deflation and took it off my list. Harvard also had a larger student body, professional schools at the graduate level, and exciting research opportunities and institutions to integrate into my experience.

My ultimate choice came down between Harvard and Stanford. It was an emotional decision to an extent since I lived right by Stanford, as I've mentioned. I basically grew up on the Stanford campus and considered it my second home. At the same time, a part of me wanted to explore new things, go to the east coast, see snow, experience the East Coast culture, and throw myself into an environment where I didn't know anyone else. I wanted to see if I could handle the challenge of being thrown into a completely new environment. And that's when I knew it was Harvard.

*7. What do you find most valuable about your Harvard education?*

Being in the Harvard environment is just amazing—part of it is the people. I'm always surrounded by peers who work hard and are very high achievers, which drives me to work harder. And not just work harder but to reach higher and see what else I can do in this world. I see my peers who are starting their businesses or political movements. Being thrown in a place like this makes me think I can achieve those things too. At a school with so much talent and resources, once you have an idea, there's not that much stopping you from implementing them. This kind of environment is ideal for incubating and generating societal change and ultimately makes you a leader.

I'm also discovering something called guidance mentorship. I learned from upperclassmen that making deep connections with peers, TFs, and grad students who may be a bit ahead of me in different life paths is a valuable resource I can tap into. Having weekly classes where I can learn under an incredible faculty member who has spent his entire life working in a particular field I didn't know had existed is mind-boggling. A definite privilege.

*8. What are you currently doing now or plan on doing in the future?*

Having just wrapped up my freshman year, I am in the process of narrowing down career options and paths. For the time being, I'm currently interested in the social sciences. To me, law is really interesting in the way human society has agreed to be bound by laws. The interaction of ethics and law, our interpretation and response to it also make for a fascinating study. Business is a new interest of mine too. Economics utilizes both the qualitative and quantitative aspects of the field. It's relevant to a lot of people and it can have a lot of impact.

*Summary of Key Points:*

1. For Students: Don't do something because you think it will look good on your applications. Just focus on taking classes and doing extracurriculars that you are really into, and those decisions will work in your favor when the time comes. Sometimes taking an international flight for a 1-day competition and returning to school the next day isn't as crazy as it seems. It's okay to take a leap of faith even though you think the odds are against you.
2. For Parents: Reading 10 to 30 books a day to your child works to instill a love of reading.
3. Sometimes taking an international flight for a 1-day competition and returning to school the next day isn't as crazy as it seems. It's okay to take a leap of faith even though you think the odds are against you.

*Review:*

With 12 AP subjects under her belt and an international harp award to top it off, Danielle was your classic overachiever. She makes everything look so easy. But she was much more than that. More than a girl who had gotten into Harvard, Princeton, and Stanford. More than a girl with a string of accolades. Danielle was a daughter who loved her parents, the girl who decorated her bedroom in pink, and a young adult who took life experiences to heart to cultivate her character, find meaning, and carve out her own path.

# The Biologist & Winter Swimmer

## Alyssa Suh

**Education:**
Harvard College, Biological Sciences and Public Health, Class of 2025
Athens High School, the Plains, Class of 2020

**GPA and Test Scores:**
GPA, (4.053/4.33)

**Extracurriculars and Awards:**
Athens High School Multicultural Club: Club Leadership Board member, The Plains Community Improvement Committee: Athens High School Representative, American Red Cross certified lifeguard, American Red Cross CPR, AED, First Aid certified, Ohio University Recreation Lifeguard, The Plains Community Logo Designer, private English tutor, children's book translator

**Hometown:**
Athens, Ohio

*What are your quirks? What do you think makes you unique?*

I'm a visual learner; I think that's why I really liked biology. I would draw diagrams, and the content would just stick in my head. For tests, I would just remember the pictures that I drew.

There is another unique thing I did in the past. When I was in the sixth grade, I swam a mile across the Columbia River in Washington State. This was in early fall, when the Columbia River actually contains freezing glacier water from the mountains. Looking back, I don't even understand how I did it.

*1. What kind of child were you growing up and what were your interests?*

I actually changed a lot from when I was little. When I first moved to the U.S. as a kid, I didn't speak any English. But, ironically, it was the other Korean kids that would bully me a lot. Because of this, I always kept my thoughts to myself, and picked up hobbies like drawing and origami, which helped develop my creative side. Later on, my hobbies extended to learning how to use Photoshop, Illustrator, and other creative skills. As I grew older, I realized I was talented athletically, which is especially valued in American culture. At one point, I had a lot of American parents coming up to me and just talking to me as if I was another adult. Sports definitely helped me build my confidence a lot and to adjust to the school environment.

I remember I was in the first grade, in PE class one day, we had to complete this obstacle course in which the teacher timed us and ranked us by time. When it was my turn, I just went through the course without giving it much thought. When everyone had their turn, and the teacher was ranking us, the teacher announced that I came in first place. I was surprised since I thought that my American classmates would be much more athletic than I was.

I guess my athleticism really came from my dad. My dad started doing triathlons after he came out of the military as a form of stress relief after work. He realized how great it was and wanted to share this experience with the rest of the family. So, when I was little, I would bike around next to my dad as he took his daily evening ride. Every evening, we would stick to this routine. Eventually, it became a weekend outing where he would take the entire family biking for a day. By the time I was in middle school, we would be doing 15K every weekend. As for swimming, it's really weird because I used to have this fear of water. That changed when I lived in Washington and joined the swim team. I have loved swimming ever since.

For fun, I also used to connect rope between trees and slackline across it with the neighborhood kids. We would also go around the neighborhood block on dirt bikes, scooters, and skateboards. I spent a lot of time outdoors.

*2. How involved were your parents in helping you to prepare for Harvard? How did they help you to learn and grow?*

They weren't very involved, to be honest, and they were really laid back in terms of raising me. I think it's because I put a lot of pressure on myself to do well in everything that I did. I didn't have a curfew during high school, and my mom would only casually send me a text at 11 p.m. to make sure I was okay. If I told her I was doing something, she trusted me. When I needed something for school or for academics, my parents were really supportive. If I needed a car ride to this activity or to an event at school, zero questions were asked. They did not have any expectations of me, and it actually seems like a miracle that I got into Harvard.

One important thing I learned from my parents was resilience in the face of hardship.

My parents are immigrants from Korea. Once they came to the States so that my dad could pursue his Ph.D., they took it upon themselves to learn English. In 2009 in Binghamton, New York, there was a shooting at the English Civic Center where my mom attended every day to learn English. Thirteen people died that day, and four were wounded. To make matters worse, it was my mom's classroom that was targeted by the gunman. So many of her closest friends and acquaintances died that day. Luckily, my mom is still alive because she happened to stay home that day to take care of me while I was sick with a stomachache. Sadly, I don't think this incident made headline news because a lot of the victims were immigrants who didn't have close family members in the States to speak up for their tragedy.

Thinking back on it now, it was an extremely difficult situation to be in, but my mom didn't show how she was suffering to the rest of the family. She was very tough. When I also saw my dad struggling to get a job because of the language barrier, I pushed myself harder because I felt like I was given a higher chance to succeed here in the U.S. Since English isn't an issue for me, I have to utilize every chance I get. This is what motivates me to do well in everything that I do.

*3. What is your most memorable memory in preparation for Harvard and what was something you experienced that you never thought you ever would?*

I basically did not think I would get into Harvard at all. If you asked me last year if I would consider applying to the school, I probably would have said no. During my junior year, my friend, who goes to Wellesley, eventually convinced me to apply. She said, "Alyssa, you should totally apply. If you don't get into Wellesley, you might get into Harvard. And then we'll be in Boston together." Looking back, I enjoyed writing my Harvard application. It was my favorite one to fill out, which probably was a telltale sign that it was the right fit. Even my grandmother would always tell me over the phone to study hard and to go to Harvard. It was the only non-Korean, renowned university that she knew. I would say to her, "Grandma, no! You can't put that pressure on me! I know you think I'm smart, but I'm not THAT smart." This conversation took place three months before I submitted my application. Once I got it in, my grandma was the happiest person on this planet. She was even telling random strangers on the street that her granddaughter got into Harvard.

*4. Study tips you have for younger students.*

For middle schoolers, or even for underclassmen in high school, I would advise figuring out what works for you. As I said before, what works for me is writing and drawing diagrams out, while for some people, it's typing up notes. You should also focus more on what you are really interested in. Yes, you should care about your grades, but you should also figure out what you're passionate about so that you can shape your application to show your interests, and to make you stand out. At the end of the day, just getting good grades isn't going to get you anywhere. You need to know what to do with that knowledge, and that comes easier with passion.

Another tip I have for everybody is to think of a certain issue in the world that drives you nuts: a problem you would like to change in society or just something that you could think about for hours. For me, that's the healthcare system in America because it sucks a lot and needs improvement. Or, if you can't find an issue you are particularly interested in, then it could be a subject in school that you find fascinating or an activity that you could easily spend hours on.

*5. What do you believe was your "X" factor to gain an admission to Harvard?*

I think I got in because I wasn't the stereotypical Asian. Not only was I ranked at the top of my class, but I was also on varsity teams for three different sports. Additionally, I live in a small township in Ohio that consists of trailer homes and a single grocery store. The fact that I was an Asian living in Appalachia was a unique story I could share when applying to schools. In one of my essays, I incorporated my experience living and doing community service in a majority-white impoverished town   in the Rust Belt region. To give you an idea of how impoverished the town was, a lot of the trailer homes had cardboard boxes affixed with duct tape as windows.

Also, I just want to say that colleges are looking for a well-rounded incoming class, and not a well-rounded person. If every applicant is a well-rounded person, then there would be a lack of diversity. I applied to different schools with this mindset, and it helped me a lot. You know how moms gossip? Korean moms, especially? The other moms said to my mom, "Let's be real, Alyssa isn't Ivy League worthy." So, when I did get accepted to Harvard, so many parents were surprised because they had a handful of kids in mind who had a shot at the top tier schools, but I was never one of those kids. I was always doing my own thing, and playing a lot of sports. I wasn't as academically inclined as my peers, but I'm so glad that my mom let me do whatever I wanted and let me pursue what I wanted to pursue.

You don't have to be good at every single subject. In the end, you're only going to major in one or two, anyway.

*6. What are some of the challenges you have faced in school?*

One challenge for me during high school was finding balance. Since I was doing a lot of time-consuming activities, like sports, trying to balance those activities with my academics was definitely challenging. By junior and senior year, there were a lot of days I would pull all-nighters to work on both schoolwork and on my college applications. That was pretty tough. At the same time, I had fallouts with friends that were in my grade. During the last two years of high school, everyone was stressed about applying to colleges and boosting their resumes, which caused a lot of competition amongst us. Moreover, because of the wide socioeconomic divide in our school, I existed in a bubble. All of the somewhat wealthy students or kids of professors took AP classes. These were the same 20 people I saw every day. For the last four years, they were the only people I could make friends with. But once junior and senior year came around, especially senior year, everyone was comparing stats with one other. Senior year was not that great for me at all.

*7. What do you find most valuable about your Harvard education?*

I am taking a gap year before starting as a freshman, but I am most excited to meet the people there, and to go to a school where everyone has unique backgrounds and life experiences. I look forward to interacting with others, and hearing everyone's stories to get to know their backgrounds. Even right now, as I'm planning my road trip with some other gap-year Harvard students, there's a kid joining from Puerto Rico. I'm already hearing different lingos and accents from all over the country, and it's mind-blowing to me how different the world is out there. Once I'm at Harvard, I'm really looking forward to making connections with all of these successful people.

*8. What are you currently doing now or plan on doing in the future?*

Although I don't really have a set plan right now, as I mentioned before, I'm really passionate about the healthcare system. I don't think

I'm going to pursue medical school, however. I don't see that in my future because I can't envision myself as a doctor. But, what I'm really interested in is biomedical engineering. I might or might not like it, but that's the route I'm trying to take. My dad once told me something that always stayed with me. He was one of those parents who would encourage his children to become doctors because he always regretted not becoming a doctor in the past. He said something along the lines of, "Isn't it so interesting that there's so much you don't know about yourself? How your own brain doesn't understand a fraction of how it works?" Whenever I am studying biology, it does feel good knowing that I'm one step closer to understanding how my body and the world around me functions.

*Summary of Key Points:*

1. For Students: Think of certain issues in the world that you would like to see remediated. Let these issues ground your passions and interests.
2. For Parents: There may be times when your child gets put down by others and told that they are not worthy to get into a certain school. During these times, remind them to pay no heed to such judgment and to not compare themselves to others.
3. Universities are looking for a well-rounded class, not a well-rounded individual. You don't have to excel in every single subject: a jack of trades is a master of none. Your application should show that you are really passionate about one or two things, and are willing to invest your finite time and energy into those pursuits.

*Review:*

Alyssa transformed from a shy child to a varsity athlete and academic to become the confident individual she is today. She learned endurance and resilience from her parents' experiences of starting a new life in the United States. These qualities allowed her to appreciate all of the opportunities her family was able to provide for her. Her positive outlook on life and drive to succeed, despite witnessing her parents' hardships as immigrants and the extreme economic divide of her community, helped her focus on areas she was genuinely interested in. Because of her strong sense of self-discipline, she gained the complete trust of her parents to continue pursuing her interests.

# The Thinker & K-Drama Translator

## Woojin Lim

**Education:**
Harvard College, Philosophy, Secondary in Government, Class of 2022
Fraser Heights Secondary, Surrey, Canada, Class of 2018

**GPA and Test Scores:**
GPA, (Unweighted (4.0/4.0))
SAT I, (1570)
APs, (Psychology, Human Geography, World History, European History, English Language & Composition, Government & Politics: United States, United States History, History of Art)

Valedictorian of High School

**Extracurriculars and Awards:**
Law/Mock Trial (courtroom simulations)
*I organized Western Canada's largest mock trial competition at the Provincial Courthouses as part of the Justice Education Society. In freshman year, I became the youngest student to win the Provincial Mock Trial competition in Victoria. I represented Canada at the world 1-on-1 mock trial championships. Also, I worked for a lobbying group against wrongful convictions and for the Canadian Bar Association.*

Speech & Debate/Politics
*At the Canadian Student Debating Federation's National Seminar, I won the Governor General's Award for being the Top National Debater in the French category. I represented my district as a youth parliamentarian at the Legislative Assembly of British Columbia and volunteered for my local minister. I competed and won awards in the national circuit, coached younger students, and adjudicated numerous international tournaments.*

Model United Nations/Model NATO
*I was one of three high school students to compete and win an award at the Global Model NATO summit alongside university students and navy officers. I chaired committees at some of Canada's largest weekend Model United Nations conferences.*

Service (Fraser Heights Secondary)
*I emceed for school-wide assemblies, coffeehouse nights, and talent shows; peer tutored students in Law 12 and Social Justice 12; wrote poems for the school-wide magazine and competed in national poetry recitation competitions; created department-wide course promotion videos for Social Studies, planned dodgeball intramurals and score-kept for after school basketball, volleyball, and badminton games as part of Senior Recreational Leadership.*

Hobbies outside of school
*Violin (orchestra, ensemble, performed for weddings and church services), taekwondo (black belt), snowboarding, film production, poetry writing, church volunteering & mission trips, translated Korean dramas into English*

*I was also enrolled in concurrent studies at Simon Fraser University while still in high school. I took classes in Introduction to Politics and Government, Philosophy of Global Justice, Modern World Literature.*

Received Governor General's Academic Medal for having the highest overall grade point average upon graduation, served as Valedictorian for the class of 2018, received Firehawk of the Year for two years consecutively (2017, 2018), National AP Scholar (2017), Principal's Honor Roll (4.0 GPA from 2014-2018), Social Studies Department Award (Top Student in Social Studies 2017), English Department Award (Top Student in English 2017), Principal's Award for Service and Leadership (2018), Parent Advisory Council Scholarship (2018).

**Hometown:**
South Korea/Canada

I have roots in Korea. I was born in Seoul but moved to Vancouver when I was five-years-old so I spent a lot of my childhood and adolescent years in Canada. I am heavily invested in K-Dramas and Korean shows and an active member of the Korean communities on campus.

*What are your quirks? What do you think makes you unique?*

Being a philosophy major, I try to take the meta-perspective and like to analyze things from various standpoints.

*1. What kind of child were you growing up, and what were your interests?*

As a child, I was always very curious. I had such an array of interests and would obsess over each one of them, understanding the merits and values of the activity and gaining a deeper understanding of who I was. In particular, I loved watching films and absorbing myself in fantasy worlds. Over the summers, when I had more time, I would watch a film a day and read a book a day.

I loved how puzzling and abstract many of these concepts explored in the books and films were. I wrote my college essay on puzzles—the solvable and the unsolvable. Some puzzles are easily solvable—like jigsaw puzzles—a problem that leads to a single, definite answer. There are other types of puzzles that don't answer or have an answer that is not so black and white. Puzzles within films allow you to glimpse into the difficult ethical or philosophical questions that the characters undergo. Rather than presenting a clear-cut solution, these films and books provide a rabbit hole of even more questions and problems to struggle with and constantly grapple with as we're leading our lives.

In the end, what I learned, or at least what I wrote about in the admissions essay, was that solving a jigsaw puzzle wasn't for the sake of solving it. For me, it wasn't the sake of its end because once you finish completing it, then the wonderment of the puzzle evaporates. The joy is in having to chase something incomplete.

*2. How involved were your parents in helping you to prepare for Harvard? How did they help you to learn and grow?*

My parents were immigrants from Korea to Vancouver, Canada, when I was just five-years-old. As an only child, they were very supportive of what I wanted to do, given that I work for the opportunities I had decided to undertake.

One summer, I went on a volunteering trip to a small town in Mexico to help the poor, impoverished communities. Over another summer, I attended film school to explore my passions in film directing. While my parents initially questioned my sincerity in pursuing this creative endeavor, I convinced them of my choice. From then on, they supported me and did everything on their part, from financial support to giving me rides every day. I can't imagine being a chauffeur for my kid because it takes a lot of time and effort and looking back. I'm grateful that they were so hands-on. Yet, also they gave me space to breathe and choose my paths and interests. From these various experiences, I was fortunate that all of these pursuits, with the support from my parents, contributed strongly to my identity.

Academically, they'd help me look up interesting classes or opportunities, and provided a big push for me to take standardized tests like SATs. I'm a writer at heart and not a multiple-choice taker. But in hindsight, I'm grateful for this push.

*3. What is your most memorable memory in preparation for Harvard, and what was something you experienced that you never thought you ever would?*

I had a lot of incredible mentors who have provided me with advice throughout the admissions process. I was once advised to look beyond the walls of high school and explore more and work towards a greater goal and not just be restricted by the opportunities around you. It made me realize what's more important than getting into like a good school like Harvard is having a better sense of who you are as a person and what you want to do later on. A Harvard degree does many things for your education and career because it serves as a seal of recognition. But this shouldn't be the end goal.

In hindsight, though, for myself, I'm glad I did not prematurely limit my possibilities by confining myself narrowly to a trade. I find I'm gaining the experiences and opening my eyes up to the world, and learning about what industries and opportunities are available to me.

As a Canadian, I've always wanted to go abroad internationally, since Vancouver is a tiny city. My high school was known for its strength in the sciences. It's got a program called Science Academy where you take two years to take college classes in between the schoolwork as an advanced acceleration in the sciences and math. So when I was in the tenth grade, I was kind of at a crossroads. Many of my peers enrolled in these programs to advance their chances of admission, even when they weren't all that interested in sciences.

I struggled with my decision because I knew that I didn't enjoy science or pure arts as much as I did the social sciences. Eventually, I decided not to enroll in the program and kind of turn away from that "traditional path," so to speak. Instead, I decided to self-study AP classes, subjects that were not offered at my school. For instance, subjects like Art History, U.S. History, European History, none of which was offered at my school. So I had to get the books myself and at night—look through the material and teach myself. But doing that was enjoyable. If I hated doing that at any point, I wouldn't have done it at all.

Another thing was I found out was that the university enrollment program was not through our high school but from the university itself. So I contacted the university and found that I could enroll in the program for free. It was open to any advanced high school students, so I took extra classes at the university. I enrolled in global justice, modern world literature, and introduction to policy and government—subjects that I loved. It was a "traditional path" in a sense, but I carved that path for myself.

*4. Study tips you have for younger students.*

I tend to write things down and scribble all of my notes on a blank sheet of unlined paper.

That gives me a lot more freedom to go wherever I want on the page. Sometimes I feel trapped by lines or certain formulas of taking notes. Seems very restrictive. On an unlined paper, how I organize things aren't just restricted or fixed by space. I can draw a diagram here, draw a chart there, or draw lines from here to there.

Another small tip! Rather than underlining or highlighting in a textbook, I use many post-it notes for note taking instead. When you're reading a book for the first time, there's a lot of nuances that you might miss. Suppose you go back and read it for the second time; if you've underlined a place during your first read, that's going to influence how you interpret it like the second, fifth, or seventh time. So, taking your notes on a post won't cloud your impression of the book on a given read.

Also, I tend to post many post-it notes everywhere—in my college dorm or the closet.

I put to-do lists, tasks, or plans to remind myself. Post-its are also useful, especially if you're writing essays, and you can rearrange the notes to play with the structure.

In terms of more general life advice, I would also say to work hard and play hard and know and have fun but relax when you have to.

Don't take the whole college process or just whatever you're doing in life too seriously. At the end of the day, like it's not a matter of life and death. Decide what's important and anchor yourself to those values. Let your values guide where you end up rather than trying to getting into Harvard for the sake of getting into Harvard. Rather than making Harvard your end goal, a place of prestige and success, make it as part of a process on your way to a passion that goes beyond that.

5. *What do you believe your "X" factor was to gain admission to Harvard?*

Rather than looking like a cluster of interests and being a well-rounded figurative ball, I think it works better to have spikes. By that, I mean to have one or two things that kind of stand out to admissions officers to make them think, wow, that's really cool and impressive.

For many people, the admissions process seems whimsical, and I think a lot of it has to do with if the officer had a good day or a nice lunch, or if they are in a good mood, or reads this application more carefully than the next. They are human, after all.

But I think, most importantly, what made my application stand out were my references. I had a chance to look through my two reference letters briefly, and I was amazed. They portrayed me so differently as

I had thought of myself. I mean, I would admit this person too! I didn't know I stood out that way to others.

6. *What are some of the challenges you have faced in school?*

The real challenge for me was easing the fact that I have a lot more free time in college and a lot less structure than I was used to. I wasn't used to being able to plan out my own time anyway I wanted. Things like how I was taking care of myself. How do I make sure that I'm eating all the time? How do I know how to squeeze in some exercise in between classes and all the socializing? Making life adjustments as a college student was more of a challenge than academic or the social aspects of Harvard life. Harvard is not as academically hard as you think.

7. *What do you find most valuable about your Harvard education?*

This is going to be very cliché, and I'm sure we're told to say this. I think Harvard preens you into saying this—but it's really the people!

It is so rare to get such a dense collection of highly motivated people from awesome backgrounds. The faculty here are straight up like rock stars, and everyone has VIP passes to meet and talk with them. They are all incredibly renowned worldwide for their work, but it's so easy to meet them in person on campus and see how their minds work, their thought processes, and even just getting a peek into that window is just incredible.

My university goes above and beyond to make guest speakers inspire sure students. Harvard brings a lot of artists and political leaders (my two core passions) to campus. I got to meet the director of Old Boy and KPOP artist Eric Nam. I also spoke with UN Secretary-General Ban Ki-Moon. We also had three presidents in a row visit the campus, and so on a certain point, I'd jokingly say, "Another president?! I don't need to go to that one."

8. *What are you currently doing now or plan on doing in the future?*

I think many of my interests (Model MUN, NATO Summit) in high school pointed me towards a career in law, government, or public service. I worked with a bunch of nonprofits, working through channels of diplomacy and getting to learn more about what compromise means.

I was working for a Minister of the Legislative Assembly one summer and witnessed the business of politics firsthand. Right now, I'm working for the United Nations. I guess I'm exploring all these possibilities and reflecting on what all of these "dots" are leading me towards.

As I'm approaching the end of my college experience. It's almost like having to go through the high school experience and reflecting on what my values are now and how they have evolved. What's my vision for life? What do I want out of life, and if I were to look back at my life from my deathbed, what would some of the shining moments make me think that this was a life worth living?

As I'm working through trying to finance myself in the future, pursuing a career path without pursuing it for the prestige of brand value only, I have bigger considerations looming in the background. I am trying to find a good balance and a compromise without losing this free-spirited nature of mine.

I'm hopefully going to be taking a gap year next year, and if things happen to open up as the pandemic comes to an end, I would like to travel a little bit and even return to Korea.

*Summary of Key Points:*

1. For Students: If your school does not offer specific classes or programs you are interested in, such as AP classes, take the initiative to study these on your own or take classes at your local community college or university to supplement your education. There are a lot of options and methods to make up for something missing from your school.

2. For Parents: What a child is interested in may seem vastly different than the last activity or extracurricular he or she was doing. If you are doubtful if any of their passions will help them achieve their goals, have students draw up a list of why

they are pursuing a certain passion so that healthy conversations can be had instead of immediately denying their pursuits.

3. Rather than making Harvard, or any university for that matter, your end goal, treating it like a stamp of prestige and success, make it as part of a process on your way to a passion that goes beyond that.

*Review:*

Woojin had an abundance of intellectual curiosity, and a lot of his time in childhood was spent thinking about concepts and theories he did not understand to satisfy his curiosity. He showed a lot of self-initiative during high school when he found that his school lacked the necessary classes and created his path apart from his other high school peers. He reminds applicants to focus on having one or two things stand out in your application instead of trying to be a well-rounded student.

# HARVARD GRADUATE
# AND PROFESSIONAL

# The Army Officer & Punctual Eater

## William Jung

**Education:**
Harvard Kennedy School, Master in Public Administration, Class of 2021
Missouri University of Science and Technology, Class of 2017
Undergraduate: United States Military Academy at West Point, Class of 2011

**Working Experience:**
Army Officer
Company Commander, 2017-2019
Project Officer (Honduras), 2013-2014
Platoon Leader (Afghanistan), 2012-2013

**Hometown:**
Santa Clarita, California

*What are your quirks? What do you think makes you unique?*

I have a pretty set mealtime. I always have to eat dinner at 5 p.m. Another quirk is that I can't walk or run and fart at the same time. In order to fart, I often pretend I have to stop and tie my shoe. Can't help it.

*1.What kind of child were you growing up and what were your interests?*

I think I've always had this fear of being average and being forgotten, if you will, while being part of a larger pack. I wanted to stand out, and part of it is because I'm the firstborn. Both my parents always relied on me to take care of my three younger siblings. My dad would always say I had to set a good example for them. So, I always wanted to distinguish myself—have my own color, if you will, and set myself apart from my peers.

As an elementary school kid, I collected a lot of baseball cards because my grandfather would take me to baseball games. I rode bikes as well, sometimes on one of those X-game types of bikes (although I did fall off of them most of the time). Both of my parents didn't enjoy being outdoors, but my grandfather loved it immensely. I remember he had a chicken coop, and we would collect eggs and clean the cages together. He also had a garden with a fish pond, too. I would help him feed the fish, and pull out the weeds from his garden beds.

Later on, my interest was in public service. I wanted to dedicate my life and talent to serving the general public. I believed that the harder I work, the better the whole of society becomes. The harder I work, the more I can protect the people who I love. The harder I work, the more I can protect our way of life. These beliefs are what propelled me to seek a life of public service.

*2.How involved were your parents in helping you to prepare for Harvard? How did they help you to learn and grow?*

My parents moved the entire family to Korea when I turned eight so that we, the children, can learn about our heritage, culture, and language. While living in Korea, my parents never stressed me out about my grades or forced me to go to after-school programs and academies (what we call *hagwons* in Korea). In fact, after ranking third from the bottom in my class, I took the initiative and asked my parents if I could attend these academies. I have to confess that I decided to attend an after-school academy because of a girl. I went to a lot of different places asking for their program brochures, but chose the one this girl I liked was attending. For the sake of appearances, I just had to make a show of it to my parents that I was considering all the options.

What my parents did, however, was talk about the "big picture." They talked about what kind of life I wanted to lead, what legacy I wanted to leave behind, and what kind of person I wanted to become. They talked about values, such as honor and integrity, to make me realize that I need to prioritize becoming a good person, rather than a successful person.

They were quite hands-off when it came to academics. When I came home with poor grades they didn't really say anything. So, obviously, grades didn't become a priority to me. In junior high, I was class president. I really admired one of my teachers, but on one midterm, I scored second from the bottom. She pulled me aside one day and scolded me, saying, "I'm disappointed in you." This comment was a turning point in my academic life, as if a light switch had gone off. After that moment, I decided to get serious about academics and become a better student.

When it came time for my college applications, having grown up in L.A., everyone talks about going to either UCLA or USC. I sat down with my dad one day and told him I wasn't really feeling these two schools, since I wouldn't know what I would do if I got in. He then talked about West Point, and said to me, "But are you man enough to go? If you want to be a great person, you have to accomplish all these things. It's going to be difficult and it's not for everybody." He kind of scratched my ego a bit like this. I applied, just to prove to him that I can, but I was fully convinced I was not going to get into West Point. But I did. So, I was like, oh crap.

As for HKS (Harvard Kennedy School), I admitted to my parents that I didn't think I could get accepted. But they were really laissez faire about this too, and said I should consider applying since I was thinking about HKS anyway. They added that I would at least live a life with no regrets if I didn't get accepted. Thanks to their encouragement, I was ultimately admitted to HKS.

*3.What is your most memorable memory in preparation for Harvard and what was something you experienced that you never thought you ever would?*

When application season came around, I was preparing all the material and studying for the tests while having a very demanding work schedule. I was working Monday through Saturday, and only had Sunday off. So, every Sunday, I would go to the library to study, but that still wasn't enough. I ultimately took a leave from work to dedicate an entire week to studying, and took the test right after that.

The most memorable thing for my Harvard application was that, because I was submitting a lot of other applications, I left HKS as the very last one. By the time I opened up the Harvard application, I was so tired from filling out the other ones. I felt like I wasn't going to even get into Harvard anyway. I remember that, for the essay portion, I wrote the whole essay in one sitting, took a bathroom break, came back, read over it just once, and just submitted it.

I ended up getting in, even though it was the application I put the least effort into.

Interestingly, HKS was not the program at Harvard I was initially interested in. Back in 2017, I came to Cambridge for a prospective student weekend for the Harvard Business School. While at HBS that weekend, I spoke with a student who was in a dual degree program with Harvard Business School and Harvard Kennedy School, and that's when I became interested in applying for HKS.

*4.Study tips you have for younger students.*

I would say backwards planning. If you have a specific day or month in mind to take a test, plan backwards from that deadline. Figure out what your weaknesses are so that you know what to study for and how to allocate time to master those subjects. I do my best to plan backwards from a test day or a certain deadline and stick to that schedule. But, of course, things happen, so I put in buffer zones in case something takes longer than I expected. Within the schedule, I also put in rest weeks or rest days to travel or to take time to get my mind off of things.

*5. What do you believe was your "X" factor to gain an admission to Harvard?*

My accomplishments as an army officer does not differ greatly from those of my peers in the Army. Like a lot of officers, I served in leadership positions leading troops into battle in Afghanistan, served as staff officer in large organizations, and served in foreign countries. I believe the difference for me was how I sought after opportunities. I was eager and motivated to manage my assignments to get the funding and approval from the Army to attend a graduate school. So, this little extra effort helped me distinguish myself from my peers. Not only that, but universities could see I was demonstrating progress over time. I had a terrible undergraduate GPA—2.99, to be exact, which is below a B average. My GRE score was just in the mid-80th percentile. But, I earned some civilian certificates throughout my career, like the PMP (Project Management Certification) and the LSSGB (Lean Six Sigma Green Belt Certification).

For Harvard Kennedy School, specifically, the big thing is public service, so you should show your potential or desire to serve the public. This could mean through a lot of community work or nonprofit work. But, for nonprofit work, be careful. I know a lot of prospective students who put down on their application that they are the founder of X, Y, Z. But the admission staff here actually look up every nonprofit. In most cases, the nonprofits are on the list, but the staff see that the applicants have no involvement. In the worst case, if they see that the organization is not even up and running, the applicant loses a lot of points. Unless it is a really established nonprofit organization, you shouldn't really put it down on your application.

For those who want to know how to develop leadership skills, you have to start somewhere. I think a lot of people think that they should become leaders overnight, to get that instant satisfaction. But if you truly want to be a leader, I think you have to learn how to be a follower first. Observe the traits of those leading you to learn what to do and what not to do. Then, it's a matter of working your way up from there.

*6. What are some of the challenges you have faced in school?*

There were two challenges I've encountered. One that's universal to most Harvard students, and the other more personal. At Harvard, there's too many options here—a buffet of options and challenges. You want to take advantage of all the options, but it's impossible. So, you have to pick and choose the one you can stick with.

The personal challenge for me was clothes.

Since I was in the Army, I had to wear uniforms all the time and I didn't have a lot of civilian clothes. But, coming here, I had to start wearing normal clothes every day which proved to be quite the challenge for me. A lot of my clothes were outdated, some even tacky, so I had to update my entire wardrobe.

*7. What do you find most valuable about your Harvard education?*

The amount of opportunities to pursue your interests through your friends, classmates, professors, and experiences and to learn more about your field. Whatever your interests are, there's definitely a way to pursue them. Whatever initiative you want to undertake, there are resources available for you so that you can get started right away. For me, because I'm an army engineer, I got to learn about cyber military intelligence logistics that I otherwise would not have been exposed to.

*8. What are you currently doing now or plan on doing in the future?*

The internship I just completed was in Chicago, where I was helping to set up COVID-19 test sites. Since I'm still on active duty, I do not have to do any internships, and even if I do, I'm not allowed to get paid for it. But I wanted this experience where I can give back, staying true to the idea of public service. We put up a lot of test sites in the suburbs of Chicago, where the local government is not very active. After I came back, I've just been reading a lot.

After my time at HKS, I'm going back to the Army. Since I'm still on active duty, I do hope to get an opportunity to go out on deployment again. They're out there fighting the fight, and I'm just here reading all day, so there is a sense of guilt. After I graduate, I want to go where I believe I can make the most difference.

*Summary of Key Points:*

1. For students: A lot of people create this mental image that getting into Harvard is unattainable. But students who attend Harvard come from all walks of life. Do not be discouraged from applying to Harvard. You will not lose anything from applying but you will lose a potential life-changing experience if you don't.
2. For parents: Give space for your kids to grow and allow them to arrive at the decision to apply to a school on their own. Talk to them about the big picture and how to grow up to be a proper member of society. When the kid is ready to talk about college, gently mention Harvard and gauge their interest to see if they even have the slightest interest in the school.
3. If you want to be a leader, learn how to be a follower first and observe the leadership qualities of those you look up to in order to learn which qualities are most valuable. Then, build your leadership skills from there.

*Review:*

William had a core value that drove all of his actions—his dedication to serving the public which he will continue to do for many years to come. This was largely in part due to his upbringing. His parents emphasized that he should focus on personal values and to think about his legacy. This core theme was evident in his applications for graduate schools. He reminds everyone to find out what your story is and to be honest with that story—not only with yourself, but with others as well.

# The Aspiring Public Policymaker & Clumsy Child

**Sophie Minsun Kang**

**Education:**
Harvard T.H. Chan School of Public Health, Public Health and Public Policy, Class of 2021
Seoul National University, Class of 2014

**Working Experience:**
Hiring Manager; Research Assistant; Regulatory Affairs, Samsung, 3 Years

**Hometown:**
Seoul, South Korea

*What are your quirks? What do you think makes you unique?*

I love meeting people and talking to them, traveling, and eating delicious food. I am often more inspired by things outside of textbooks.

*1.What kind of child were you growing up and what were your interests?*

As a child, I would constantly come home injured after playing outside. I wasn't necessarily frail, but I had to go to the orthopedics a lot because I would often break a bone here and there. There was one time where I hit a glass door so hard that I had to get 300 stitches. Since I went to the doctor's office and hospital so many times, I was able to meet many doctors and be exposed to the hospital environment from a young age. And, naturally, I became more intrigued about the human body. In elementary school, I would read picture books about the human body, and memorize the names of muscles and bones.

My interest became very serious when my grandfather died of lung cancer when he should still have had quite a few years ahead of him. I realized for the first time that a disease could lead to the loss of a precious person in your life. Even though I was still a kid, I dreamed of developing cancer treatments and vaccines as an adult. It definitely did help that there were many doctors in my family to inspire me, so I grew up respecting their ability to save lives. Although my dreams have changed many times, as often occurs with children, most were linked to saving lives in some way, shape, or form.

When I became a little bit older, I naturally gravitated towards math and science as a student. Within those subjects, I especially loved to study living things. I could see how my body worked, and I wanted to learn more, so I majored in biological sciences in college. Looking back, I think I've always been interested in the topic of how to live a "healthy" life.

Though I'm not on the path of a scientist or a doctor like I dreamed of as a child, the general idea is still there: helping people lead healthier lives.

*2.How involved were your parents in helping you to prepare for Harvard? How did they help you to learn and grow?*

My parents have always been my strongest supporters. I am thankful that they always asked for my opinion. Whether it was learning to play a musical instrument, ballet, or school, they asked. I was never forced to learn something I didn't want to learn.

My parents were also great teachers. Even though they were both incredibly busy with work, they never hesitated to teach me concepts I didn't understand. I have a memory from back in elementary school where, for the first time, I encountered a set of math equations that seemed daunting. I couldn't understand them, so I asked my mother for help. She kindly explained to me how to solve them, and stayed by my side until I solved all the problems. When I looked up at the clock, it was already way past 5 a.m. Whereas I could go right back to sleep, my mother, on the other hand, was a doctor and had to wake up at 7 a.m. to go straight to work. In another instance, when I was in high school, I didn't know much about history or sociology because I was a STEM major. I asked my father for help, and he was able to explain it to me better than any of my teachers.

I'm really thankful that my parents always believed in me and cheered me on. Even when I dropped out of my Ph.D. program and joined a company, my parents supported my choice. Never in my life have they nagged at me to study. They embraced every choice that I made, and took the time to know what it was that I wanted in life.

*3.What is your most memorable memory in preparation for Harvard and what was something you experienced that you never thought you ever would?*

I initially joined Samsung as a researcher. I had majored in bioscience, but once I entered the company, I was suddenly assigned to the human resource team. I ended up doing something that had nothing to do with what I studied to do. However, as I met a variety of people and foreigners, alike, I was exposed to a lot of foreign public health cases that were not as developed in Korea. The only knowledge I developed in college was science-related, but I think I was able to see and experience the bigger world through that position.

I'm currently studying public health policy because I believe that people can live healthy lives through not only the development of science, but also through policy. That's why I think my work experience helped me realize what it was that I wanted to do, and how I wanted to move forward with it.

I suddenly felt the urge to study more before it was too late. I knew that if I went abroad to study, there would be a lot of things I would have to give up, but I wanted to find a way to satisfy my intellectual curiosity. I was able to gain courage after seeing many of my colleagues seek out graduate schools to pursue their dreams.

*4.Study tips you have for younger students.*

When I was a high school student, Korean entrance exams were very difficult, so I would pull all-nighters too many times than I would like to admit. I personally thought that the time put into studying correlated with the test score. Because I wasn't a genius, I had to try harder and would go out early in the morning to solve one language test sheet a day. For someone who likes to sleep in, I forced myself to wake up super early and be the first one at school during my third year of high school. I don't necessarily have a secret for how I got into Seoul National University, but I think I was able to raise my chances by slowly reducing time out of my sleep schedule.

As for preparing for the GRE for my grad school applications, it was my first time taking such a test. I stumbled upon a lot of unfamiliar words that I had a hard time memorizing. There are a lot of people who stress over getting high GRE scores here in Korea.

However, in America, they look at a variety of aspects. In addition to the score, they also look at extracurricular activities, volunteer work, etc. I think international applicants in general are too focused on their scores. Instead, some of that time would be better spent if people took the time to consider what and why they would like to study, and additionally prepare some activities to support your story.

In my case, biology and public health policy are subjects that are slightly different, so I had to present an explanation as to why I decided to steer my path towards public health. Before submitting your application, it is crucial that you take some time to think about why you want to study a certain subject in order to explain your motivations well to others.

*5.What do you believe was your "X" factor to gain an admission to Harvard?*

Most of my college classmates decided to either pursue a Ph.D. in science and engineering, or to attend medical school. But, I decided to go into the workforce to gain experience through working for a company. I was crazy busy working for three years, but I was able to meet so many new people and mentors. I used to believe that the development of science could change the world. But, through my work experience, I came to realize that there's a need for a system to give people access to healthcare first. For example, when I was in high school, a cervical cancer vaccine was developed for the first time. However, because the price of the vaccine was expensive, and little was known about the vaccine, many people missed the timeframe of getting vaccinated. But, these days, people have learned a lot about the vaccine, and I've even heard that the Korean government is giving free vaccinations to twelve-year-old girls. In this way, I realized the importance of health policies, and decided to apply to Harvard's graduate program to learn more.

I think the decisive reason why I was able to get into Harvard is the experiences I mentioned earlier. Currently, the Master of Public Health (MPH) program requires more than two years of work experience in order to apply. I was also able to compile a lot of advice from people I came to know through my job.

*6.What are some of the challenges/ hardships you have faced in school?*

English is probably a stress that will never go away.

At a school like Harvard that has a lot of discussion-based classes, these classes may be a struggle for students who have grown up cramming in schools like in Korea. Even if they understand the content, there are times where they may have nothing to say.

My American classmates are already so good at talking and comfortable participating in discussions, but with my level of English proficiency and poor discussion skills, I am naturally put at a disadvantage. Sometimes, I can't find anything to say in class, and other times, when I do, I can't get myself to properly form it into words. Back in Korea, I never felt dumb amongst other people. Yet, here in America, when I can't get myself to speak in class, I feel lesser than others. In that aspect, there were times where I felt a bit insecure and ashamed. There were barely any instances where I directly received stress from other people, but rather, there's a lot more self-induced stress due to low self-esteem. And, these days, there are a lot of foreigners stressing over visa and political issues.

*7.What do you find most valuable about your Harvard education?*

First of all, there are so many great professors. Through my studies, I received a lot of fresh and thoughtful information when senators and congressmen came to give lectures. Also, the alumni network is tightly established, so I can get help if I look for a few seniors who have the information I need in the direction I would like to go.

Also, when I compare my experience from those that I had in the school I attended in Korea, I think it's better to learn in an environment where the students are put on equal footing as the professors, rather than through a hierarchical relationship. The professors at Harvard I've studied under try to the best of their abilities to explain new information.

*8.What are you currently doing now or plan on doing in the future?*

I used to work for a Korean pharmaceutical company, so I would like to work for an American pharmaceutical company with a more developed market. After graduation, I want to apply my studies at a pharmaceutical company, and learn more about the U.S.'s pharmaceutical laws and the kinds of policies the FDA are implementing, since it's such a regulated industry.

*Summary of Key Points:*

1.  For Students: If your personal, academic, and professional experiences are different than the intended program you are trying to apply for, take the time to solidify the reasons why you want to pursue a certain subject or field, and make the connections that way.
2.  For Parents: Although most parents may not have the time or patience to sit down with their child into the early hours of the morning to help with their child's schoolwork, just showing interest in their studies and offering help can make a child feel assured that their struggles and questions can be expressed.
3.  Students come from a variety of cultural backgrounds and education systems, and may not feel comfortable speaking freely in class or joining class discussions, at first. It is not only important to acknowledge these differences, but also to find ways to encourage participation.

*Review:*

Sophie let her childhood interest in saving lives through science lead her to where she is today. What was also striking was her parents' dedication to helping Sophie understand her schoolwork, even if it means losing a good night's sleep. Her parents also never pushed anything onto Sophie, and was always mindful of their child's thoughts and feelings. Because of her supportive parents, Sophie was able to be honest with them when she felt that staying on the Ph.D. path was not right for her, and that she would instead benefit from gaining experience working at a company.

# The Aspiring Lawyer & Master of Deconstruction

## Victor Roh

**Education:**
Harvard Law School, Class of 2021
University of Notre Dame, Bachelor of Business Administration: Management, summa cum laude, Class of 2016

**GPA and Test Scores:**
LSAT, (171/180)
GMAT, (770/800)

**Working Experience:**
Summer Associate, Davis Polk & Wardwell LLP, New York, NY, June 2020-Present
Bridge to BCG Fellow, Boston Consulting Group, New York, NY, June 2020
Intern, The World Bank Group, Washington DC, May 2019-July 2019
Analyst, Deloitte Consulting LLP, New York, NY, July 2016-July 2017
Summer Analyst, Deloitte Consulting LLP, Chicago, IL, May 2015-July 2015
Commander's Adjutant, Republic of Korea Army (Attachment to the United Nations Command Korea), Panmunjom, Paju, Gyeonggido, August 2011-May 2013

**Hometown:**
Daegu, South Korea (New York City, NY at heart)

I was born in Daegu, Gyeongsang-do, but I've never lived in one place for more than 3 years. I moved from Korea to Australia to live there for a short period of time. Then I moved to Chicago, New York, and Boston, in that order.

Of those places, I think New York is the city most close to my heart. New York was where I started my first job, established my values as a mature adult, and started wanting to become a lawyer. Even after I graduate from law school, New York is where I want to start my career as a lawyer.

*What are your quirks? What do you think makes you unique?*

Despite my law school credentials, I have a lot of interests that are not law related. My undergraduate minor was in art and photography. When I was a business student, I was really interested in computer science.

*1.What kind of child were you growing up and what were your interests?*

Growing up, I loved to make things. As a young kid, I showed the qualities of an architect, a builder, and an engineer altogether. I never liked purchasing pre-built toy sets, and preferred building my own designs with Lego pieces. Instead of playing Starcraft straight out of the box, for example, I took the initiative to create my own maps and objects with custom-coded triggers in order to create my own version of the game. This mindset that valued designing a new solution trained me to think in a very specific way. I developed the tendency to break anything, from ideas to programs to machines, into elemental pieces of logical processes that are bound together. As a result, I became a logical thinker who could analyze and understand complex concepts.

In the legal world, every legal problem must be broken down into the very basic elements which interact with one another intricately. Likewise, a problem starts as a big concept.

*2.How involved were your parents in helping you to prepare for Harvard? How did they help you to learn and grow?*

Because law school is a graduate school, my parents didn't give me any substantial help. But, what helped me the most was their infinite faith and support. I was actually preparing for an MBA (Master of Business Administration) because my undergraduate major was management, and my first job was in consulting. I had already even taken the GMAT. But, one day, I decided to call my parents and told them, "I don't want to go for an MBA. I'm going to law school." Despite the short notice and the extra year that I would need to prepare, my parents supported my decision. The decision must have been hard for my parents to accept with ease since it was a pivot, but their unlimited support and faith allowed me to comfortably pursue my decision during the preparation process.

Even in school, my parents rarely gave me a firm "no" as an answer. I never asked them things that were completely outrageous, but I have asked for a lot of things I was interested in, namely hobbies that were not necessarily related to studying. I would ask questions like, "Dad, I really want to take pictures. Do you think you could buy me a camera?" or, "I really want to play the guitar. Can I get lessons?" If I wanted to do something, they wouldn't question my interests, but rather, support me and tell me to do my best.

*3.What is your most memorable memory in preparation for Harvard and what was something you experienced that you never thought you ever would?*

The American law school admission process is quite similar to the Korean one. While other factors are considered, GPA and LSAT scores are really important. To get into Harvard Law School, it is advised that you score within the one percent range of all LSAT takers. I was so nervous the day before my LSAT that I couldn't sleep at all. I actually failed that attempt because I was so tired from staying up all night. Because one can only take the LSAT four times a year, if I failed a test, I would have to wait three months before my next attempt.

But even in that important time period, what I remember the most is how I handled the situation. With so much stress and the deadline approaching, my first priority was getting into the right state of mind. I would remind myself, "Don't worry about it now. I can worry about it later when I fail the exam." This really helped me control my stress level instead of constantly worrying about the possibility of failing.

When I graduated from the top of my class in college, my professors actually recommended that I should go to law school. I told them that I would rather return for a doctorate than go to law school. But, as it turns out, life is something you can't predict. While consulting, I realized that law played a big part of my business group and even limited my scope of work. There was an instance when I was dispatched to Kentucky to carry out an M&A work project for two months, but I had to pack up and come back within a month. Our project was suspended after the Washington D.C. Circuit Court held that the merger was in violation of an antitrust law. Through this direct experience, studying law piqued my intellectual curiosity.

Harvard Law School has a lot of students coming in with their own strong "mission." There are many students who want to solve the social missions of the Civil Rights Movement, LGBTQ rights, and poverty. Though my mission wasn't as ambitious as theirs, I think I had a strong desire to learn to build bridges between the business world and the legal one.

*4.Study tips you have for younger students.*

There is a common saying in the Korean army, "In training, train as if you are in the real action. When in real action, act as if you are in training." For me, it was really important to keep this phrase in mind at all times. When I was in high school, university, and law school, I always studied at a very consistent pace, and spread out my workload for the entire semester. Because I did this, I tended to relax physically and mentally a bit when the exam period was around the corner, rather than cramming everything. So, during the days leading up to the fateful exam period, I would tell my friends who were staying up all night at the library, "I'm done for the day. Peace out." This way, I would "flex" by leaving the library at 8 p.m. instead of at 4 or 5 a.m. like the others.

Tests put a lot of pressure on studying for anybody, but it's a good habit to study little by little in order to minimize stress and to maximize longevity.

Also, it is really important to constantly reward yourself. After final exams or completing a task, you should treat yourself with a small reward.

*5.What do you believe was your "X" factor to gain an admission to Harvard?*

I finished my military service at the DMZ truce zone. I was in a military uniform in the Joint Security Area (JSA), facing the other side in sunglasses. I often saw North Korean soldiers and North Koreans commoners from only 5 to10 meters away. Sometimes, I used to see smoke hit the hills beyond Panmunjom. I later found out the smoke

was coming from the second largest city in North Korea, Kaesong. It's really dark in North Korea at night, but there were some places where the lights came on and looked like dots. The source of the lights was the Gaesong Industrial Complex that Hyundai E&C invested in. I was deeply impressed when I learned that a private sector investment, in this case a South Korean one, can create public goods and make a social impact. This realization naturally led me to an interest in understanding the framework that promotes as well as constrains the private sector and the economy overall: the law.

Like how my personal experience greatly impacted me, another advice I would like to give for students and applicants is to look back on the five to ten years of their own lives. Relive old stories, and think of lessons from those experiences. You will come to realize that there is an underlying story that weaves together all of those experiences, one that speaks to your passions and aspirations.

Realistically, because law schools tend to place heavier emphasis on high grades and test scores, aspiring law school applicants should be aware of its significance. However, if you look at my own admission score, it's only average in comparison to all of the other Harvard Law School students. Though there are some students here with really great scores, I think I was able to stand out from other applicants because of my unique story. I was able to successfully organize and convey where I came from, who I am, and then where I planned to go after.

*6. What are some of the challenges you have faced in school?*

There are so many insanely outstanding students at Harvard Law School. I was so intimidated when I first stepped into class with the thought that I was going to school with future presidents, senators, and Supreme Court justices. I was studying with so many talented individuals who would most likely lead the U.S. Justice Department in the future. In actuality, however, they were all extremely humble with their abilities and achievements. I think it helped me overcome my imposter syndrome when I finally realized that I saw myself as less than what others thought of me.

Of course, there is a lot of competition due to the nature of a law school in general, but the competition is slightly subdued because it is Harvard. For Harvard Law School, the admissions process filters out the best students so you can practically get a job wherever you want. If you want to go to a law firm, it's totally possible. If you want to be a law clerk, you can go for that as well. That's why there is no pressure to beat out classmates for jobs. That being said, the students are all very hard-working, so there seems to be a competition of pride that exists even amongst such a well-accomplished community.

If you want to simply join a law firm, you can pass by with just your grades from your first year. But, if you are aspiring to be a legal academic or a law clerk, you need to manage and maintain your grades all for all three years,

*7.What do you find most valuable about your Harvard education?*

Law is such a broad topic that even those who have been working as lawyers for ten to twenty years often say, "I still can only understand half of what I'm saying or hearing." There really seems to be no end to learning. Harvard Law School has a bar exam pass rate of nearly 100%, so instead of training students to perform well on the bar exam, classes train students on how to think like a lawyer so that they can tackle any problem, including those they initially do not comprehend.

At Harvard Law School, during lectures in the first year, students and professors share a discussion-based class where students debate over the interpretation of each law principle for 70 minutes. We are given the creative freedom to have our own opinions, and the professor often cold calls on students to express their thoughts. The professor rarely explains the principle until the last 10 minutes of the class when he or she finally reveals the modern interpretation of the law.

If I benefitted anything from studying at Harvard, I think it would definitely be the network. It is a really good place to build a network with so many talented people who all will become prominent leaders and chairs of top legal offices in the future.

*8.What are you currently doing now or plan on doing in the future?*

My plan is to start working at a law firm in New York. In fact, the reason I chose non-law-related internships, such as at the World Bank and BCG, during law school was because I wanted to have various experiences in the working environment. I think it's my way of finding what I like to do.

When I was young, I would often change my dreams. Even when I became an adult, I decided that I wanted to become a lawyer at the very last minute. The moral of the story is that I don't have to stick to one field. I think it is important to take a look at my changing interests over time.

That's why, even as a law school graduate, I don't think that I will tie myself down to one field or turn my back on new opportunities.

*Summary of Key Points:*

1. For Students: If you have the aspiration to apply to a law school, put in the time and effort to maintain your GPA and LSAT test scores. Particularly, if you want to gain acceptance into Harvard Law School, you preferably have to get within the one percent range of all LSAT test takers.
2. For Parents: A student may suddenly decide to switch careers that seem unrelated to the one they were originally pursuing. Instead of worrying about the consequences that may come with making last-minute decisions, it is important to help them realize how their past experiences can contribute to the new professional and academic journey they are about to pursue.
3. A benefit of going to top law schools, such as Harvard Law School, is that the admissions process filters out the best students. In this regard, competition for jobs is not a major concern upon graduation.

*Review:*

Victor realized his childhood experiences of designing his own games and Lego structures played a significant role in developing his logical thinking skills to understand complex concepts. Such reasoning skills would eventually benefit him as a law student. His military experience at the DMZ truce zone between North and South Korea allowed him to see the social and economic impact of laws. This unique experience was a pivotal factor that made Victor stand out amongst other applicants. He reminds everyone that it is completely okay to change fields or have interests in many fields because a new direction or a new choice in life can provide welcome opportunities.

# The Linguist & Dancer

## SeonMin Park

**Education:**
Northern Arizona University PhD, Applied Linguistics, Class of 2015
Harvard Graduate School of Education EdM, Language and Literacy, Class of 2011
Sungkyunkwan University, Bachelor of Arts in English Language and Literature, Class of 2007

**Working Experience:**
EFL Curriculum Director at Korea Advanced Institute of Science and Technology (KAIST)

**Hometown:**
Seoul, South Korea

*What are your quirks? What do you think makes you unique?*

If there was one word to describe me, it would be, "bridge." Let me explain. I really enjoy being in new places, meeting new people, and learning new things. I think that's why I end up playing the "bridge" role a lot. I work at KAIST (Korea Advanced Institute of Science and Technology), a university known for its STEM programs, but I was a humanities major. Over time, I had to figure out how to bring the humanities and the sciences together through the curriculum and make the connections or, "bridge," between them.

*1. What kind of child were you growing up, and what were your interests?*

A lot of people thought I was shy at first glance, but my parents told me I was always a bright and talkative child. My father still has a distinct memory of me going up to complete strangers at the department store just to say hello to them. I was also a big fan of music and dance and much later on, during my graduate studies at Harvard, three of my Harvard friends and I were invited to perform a Miss A concert from a Korean-American organization and even made headlines. Look it up on YouTube if you have the time! One of my other passions was calligraphy, which I've won national awards for. I also did piano, writing, swimming, etc. I not only loved to learn new things but wanted to learn them as fast as possible.

As a kid growing up in South Korea, I became interested in American culture when I said, "hello," to a blue-eyed American for the very first time—almost like a scene out of a movie. It was my first time using English and I felt like I had discovered this new secret language and I needed to know more. Learning English became one of my hobbies after that.

*2.How involved were your parents in helping you to prepare for Harvard? How did they help you to learn and grow?*

My parents were not the ones to tell me to study abroad. In fact, it was actually one of my teachers who suggested that I should put in applications for universities in the United States.

I don't think I remember consulting with my parents first. I just kind of decided on my own that I would apply, and I got straight to it. My parents watched me make my decision silently, and I could feel them peering over my shoulder as I browsed through various university websites. Although they didn't say anything, I just felt their trust whenever they were around. Since I majored in English as an undergraduate, I really wanted to go abroad to actually use and study the language 24/7. Interestingly, when I was preparing my graduate school applications, my parents neither supported nor opposed my decision. In the end, I felt incredibly lucky to have been accepted to Harvard, Columbia, and a lot of other great universities. Of the schools in this list, I eventually chose Harvard's Graduate School of Education Language and Literacy program. Of course, once they knew of my decision, we celebrated to the fullest extent. Although my parents did not have a huge role in the decision-making process, as my parents, they raised me to be the person I am today, and that is a significant reason why I was able to achieve all these goals.

*3.What is your most memorable memory in preparation for Harvard, and what was something you experienced that you never thought you would?*

Back then, I was racing against the clock. I had such a limited time to prepare for my application for Harvard, and looking back, I honestly do not know how I did it. I started in September and finished by the end of November, so two and a half months. In that timeframe, I finished my TOEFL and GRE exams, filled out the necessary applications, put my signature here and there, took liberties with my coffee intake, and pressed one of the scariest, yet most thrilling words in the English dictionary, *submit*.

I remember studying really intensely until my eyes felt like they would pop out—even harder than I did in high school. From 9 o'clock in the morning, to 9 o'clock at night, I would form study groups with my friends and just hit the books.

It was to the point where I would be sitting in the front seat and my friends sitting behind would look and say, "It looks like SeonMin's on fire from back here." I had no choice but to concentrate as if my seat was on fire because I just didn't have the time.

That period of just intensely focusing on the task before me and getting something done got ingrained within me somehow. It was this same perseverance that allowed me to get into Harvard, complete my Masters at Harvard, and finish my Ph.D. Although no one really has enough time, the whole experience gave me the confidence that I really can do anything if I just maximize my concentration level.

*4.Study tips you have for younger students.*

I was appointed by the Department of Education in South Korea as a talented volunteer and I gave free career lectures to students from time to time. The number one thing I always tell the students is to look for things that they like to do or do well. Even though you can't get rid of the fact that you should always strive for good grades at school, there's so much more to learning than just worrying about your grade point average.

In my career lectures, I ask my students to make a simple three columned table. I ask them to list their top ten favorite things, things they do well, and things they dislike. They don't necessarily have to write down an academic subject. If they like cooking, they can write that down, or if they like taking care of their younger sibling, it belongs in the table as well. This exercise gives the students a chance to write without restrictions. It's a good exercise to try at least once for everybody. You have to discover your own likes and dislikes early on to eventually navigate your career path.

Also, for any applicants out there who are thinking about applying to graduate schools, never assume that only people born into wealth or with a lot of time to prepare for applications can go to Harvard or any top tier university. Of course, someone with a lot of time and financial resources may have a higher chance of being accepted. But, even for my own case it really only took two and a half weeks to apply. It really was a blur. I would have to say my expenses were small with zero outside help from any private institutions or academies other than the application and testing fees. Also, the good news is, once you are accepted, there are so many scholarship opportunities and Harvard is so generous with their aid packages so people with various financial standings are able to qualify for a lot of scholarships.

*5.What do you believe was your "X" factor to gain an admission to Harvard?*

Before I left to study abroad, I looked back on my 5-10 years of personal and professional experiences to compose my SOP (Statement of Purpose) and CV for Harvard. From my experiences teaching English in Singapore, England, Ireland, Korea, etc., involvement in volunteering activities, and more, I realized that I filled up a lot of leadership positions and stacked up a good amount of experiences over those past 5 to 10 years.

By no means did I have a certain strategy or have the intention of working at particular places just so that it could "look good" on my resume. All of the activities I did really just came naturally to me. I presented my experiences and stories in a way that showed that I really loved what I was pursuing.

In terms of standardized tests, having a higher score will not really help you that much, in my opinion. I've seen a lot of students with a perfectly decent GRE score but still wanting to retake the exam over and over again just to incrementally improve. Instead, you should focus on your SOP (editing it 10 to 20 times), your experiences, and other supplemental materials in your application that will have the greatest impact. This was something I did not fully appreciate until I was accepted.

*6. What are some of the challenges you have faced in school?*

The banking system.

I always tell the story of the first time I was at an American bank whenever I get asked this. Besides learning English in the EFL context, hands down I would have to say one of the most difficult obstacles I encountered once I arrived in the States was my lack of familiarity in this new culture I found myself in.

For the life of me, I did not understand why it would only take me 5 to 10 minutes to set up a bank account in Korea, but it would take 5 hours to set up an account in the States. But, seeing that this was just the way things were done, I decided to make light of the situation and struck up a conversation with the bank teller that became really engaging. Just with that one instance, I came to the conclusion that while Korean employees are very business-like and efficient in handling affairs, the workers in the U.S. are very sociable and take the time to get to know you personally.

The same principle can be applied to the doctor's office, post office, and grocery stores. But not the DMV. No, definitely not the DMV.

*7. What do you find most valuable about your Harvard education?*

The number one thing is the people you will meet there.

While I was at Harvard, I attended various events and seminars as a student council representative of the Graduate School of Education in the Harvard Korean community. The experience of exchanging interdisciplinary practices with your peers was something that stood out to me during my entire academic career. Everybody was just so excited to bounce ideas off of one another, collaborate on projects, and really just to learn from one other.

During high school and my undergraduate studies, there were so many times where I would give up on sleep, drink out of a bottomless pit of coffee, read hundreds of pages, and attend early morning classes. It was stressful to say the least. But at Harvard, even if I pulled an all-nighter or had to attend early morning classes, things were just so much more fun and I felt more alive. Maybe it's because I was surrounded by people who were extremely positive and self-driven. By no exaggeration, I enjoyed every single moment and experience there.

*8. What are you currently doing now or plan on doing in the future?*

For now, I will continue to find ways to help students and figure out what they really need out of their education system. As the curriculum director of KAIST's EFL program, through research and lectures, I will find new ways on how to maximize the limited time students have to learn English. I've also been recently put in charge of a project called STAR-MOOC, which is supported by the Korean government, and offers open lectures to many schools in the country.

I also teach classes on Coursera! My courses are called Big Data and Language. Though I've taught all kinds of students, for these courses, I am teaching students who majored in computer engineering on how to analyze text data or teaching students who majored in language arts the important skill of how to analyze big data in this day and age. Volunteering as an educator is something I can see myself doing for many years to come, so I will continue to give lots of free lectures and courses on how someone can jump start their career. This is how I met so many elementary, middle, and high school students who have later said that my advice for them has helped them in so many ways. This is something that I feel incredibly lucky to hear as an educator. Even if, at the end of the day, I am able to change the heart and mind of one student out of all that I meet, then I've done my job.

*Summary of Key Points:*

1. For Students: Feel like you don't have time to put together an application for graduate school? With dedication, completing all the application requirements (and testing) can be achieved even within two months. For extra motivation, find people you can study with.
2. For Parents: Help your child be prepared for culture shock. Remind him or her to embrace it, then he or she can adapt to any environment a lot more quickly. But nothing prepares anybody for the lines and customer service at the DMV.
3. Focus on your Statement of Purpose and your CV rather than your standardized test results. These factors will help you give the edge to an acceptance rather than a score that has been increased by a few points.

*Review:*

SeonMin's ability to just focus on the goals and tasks at hand really helped her achieve what she had intended to do in a short period of time. What is more apparent was that she had a great passion and inclination for education, especially educating the youth in her community. Her time spent giving free lectures to young students shows that your knowledge and skill sets can have a positive impact on at least one other person in this world.

# The Techie Lawyer & Lego Builder

## Alan Gyehyun Kim

**Education:**
Harvard Law School, Class of 2021
MIT, Materials Science & Engineering PhD, Class of 2016
UC Berkeley, (Departmental Citation Winner), Class of 2010

**Working Experience:**
Semiconductor Engineer, Silicon Valley

**Hometown:**
South Korea

My home country will always be Korea, since I spent most of my childhood there. I was born in Korea, and lived there until my sophomore year in high school. At that time, I moved to China with my family, where I completed the rest of high school. After high school, I decided to go to the U.S. for college.

*What are your quirks? What do you think makes you unique?*

I tend to focus a lot on planning and working sequentially. I am the type to stress out if a deadline is approaching and things don't go as planned. So, I try to start and finish my work as soon as possible. Just in case, I make a thorough "plan B" as a backup.

*1. What kind of child were you growing up and what were your interests?*

I was a quiet kid growing up. I didn't have a penchant for sports , so I ended up spending a lot of time at home.

Naturally, my hobbies became reading and Lego building (although, admittedly, I felt that my quiet personality and dislike for sports put me at a disadvantage later on). Through my hobbies, I was able to create complex structures, and read a variety of books that developed my study skills in multiple subjects. Of all the books I read in my childhood, I especially liked one titled *Samgukji* and read different versions of it dozens of times. In addition to reading, I started playing the violin when I was six, and spent my school days doing various orchestral activities.

*2. How involved were your parents in helping you to prepare for Harvard? How did they help you to learn and grow?*

After middle school, my parents became rarely involved in my studies. Rather than my parents approaching me first, I instead went to my parents for help whenever I needed assistance with academics. My parents never told me what to do, but still watched over me and took interest in areas I needed extra help. I think I was able to work more actively by myself thanks to my parent's unwavering support.

*3. What is your most memorable memory in preparation for Harvard and what was something you experienced that you never thought you ever would?*

The first midterm exam I took in middle school was also my first time taking an exam that would determine my class ranking. Thanks to my parents' full support (and a little bit of luck), I was ranked first out of my entire class. I believe that this strong start paved the way to my success. After ranking first, I was warned that it is difficult to maintain the top spot. After hearing this, I didn't ever want to lose that spot. I tried even harder, eventually graduating at the top of my entire middle school. After this achievement, I was motivated to move on to study at a more rigorous place. I thus decided to attend Daewon Foreign Language High School. My experience studying there sparked my dream of studying abroad in the U.S. My personality changed, as well! I became more adventurous. I found myself wanting to try new things and attempt challenges head on. I think my educational background and newfound personality had big impacts on reaching my goals.

*4. Study tips you have for younger students.*

There is no "secret" that works for everyone. Instead, I think it is more important for students to practice setting specific long-term goals, and learning to continually move forward with the plan. Be sure to set aside time for breaks to avoid getting burnt out. Planning ahead will help students figure out study approaches that best suit their learning style and follow through with their goals.

Moreover, don't miss out on diverse experiences in order to solely focus on academics early on in your life. The best universities, including Harvard, nowadays all no longer select "students who only excel academically." Instead, such schools tend to select students with unique experiences that accompany their high grades. Also, it's not just about getting into the best universities like Harvard. That shouldn't be the end goal. It's more important for you to understand how going to these schools will play out in your future, and what kind of studies you would like to pursue there. Having a background of many different experiences can help you have a more concrete idea of your future.

Furthermore, you should always keep in mind that studying is a "cooperative" activity. Evidently, the competition for admission to prestigious universities is fierce. In the past, it was easy for me to see my friends as competitors. For this reason, I was often reluctant to help out others. But through personal experience, I was able to realize that there are limits to studying alone, and that it can actually be more difficult.

In order to exceed your limits, you need to be able to make up for your flaws and shortcomings that you may not see by yourself. By helping one another, you can help identify areas you need to improve upon along the way. For example, think twice before turning away a friend who needs help understanding a concept, even if you see that individual as a competitor. Opt to be a good friend, and explain the concept. This will benefit your long-term growth. Even though I was able to understand certain concepts through studying by myself, there were a lot of instances in which I had trouble. Interestingly, the process of teaching the concepts to my friends in detail allowed me to gain a better grasp on the material.

On a similar note, it is more important to find a study partner that clicks well with you. The world has become so complicated that people who would objectively be considered geniuses, like Isaac Newton and Leonardo da Vinci, can no longer exist. To unravel the future big discoveries of this world, people need to collaborate with others that have expertise in areas they lack. I want students to start seeing their surrounding peers as future partners, rather than as competitors.

It is a pity that more people aren't interested in helping others. In fact, I am currently running a study-related YouTube channel called 멘토스TV (Mentors TV) to help as many people as possible by sharing various information of my own. I am hoping that the students who watch my videos will begin to sympathize with others, and aim to be part of a society where everyone helps one another grow.

*5. What do you believe was your "X" factor to gain an admission to Harvard?*

I graduated from college as an engineering major, and went on to get a Ph.D. in Materials Science & Engineering at MIT. I decided to go to Harvard Law School to pursue a career in the field of technology law. Because it is rare for a person with an engineering degree and work experience in Silicon Valley to attend law school, I think this factor helped me out a lot.

I also want to say that if you can compile the steps you have taken thus far to achieve your dream and present this to the admissions officers, your unique story can become your strongest asset in differentiating yourself from others. In this regard, I hope that students will not miss out on opportunities to gain valuable experiences because they were too focused on studying.

Though I was an engineer, I was also interested in finance and management, so I studied consulting and CFA on my own. I felt that law school admissions strongly preferred applicants to have other substandard knowledge in the legal profession. Of course, school grades and entrance exams are important. That being said, it seems that experience and unique skills are much more valued in the Harvard community, which is reflected in their admissions process. For example, I was able to get into Harvard Law School with a below average LSAT score because of my unique background as an engineer.

*6. What are some of the challenges you have faced in school?*

Many people think that going to Harvard will solve all their future problems and lead them to great careers, but frankly, this is not the truth. Grades are still important and job interviews still exist, but the biggest hardship I felt was something called "imposter syndrome," or the extreme pressure you feel from being surrounded by outstanding people.

Everyone accepted into Harvard got in because they all had an outstanding quality. But the longer we co-exist together, we start to compare ourselves to others with "greater" specs. Comparing ourselves to others makes us feel like we are falling behind, thereby creating a cycle of stress and anxiety.

It's a common reality to be constantly surrounded by the best of the best. I had to go so far as limiting interactions with other students as much as possible in order to stop myself from comparing my accomplishments with others. I avoided the library because I thought watching other students studying under stress would stress me out too. It ended up working out because I was able to push ahead at my own pace, eventually overcoming obstacles and receiving good grades.

*7. What do you find most valuable about your Harvard education?*

For one, having "Harvard" on your resume is something that cannot be ignored. When I'm looking for a job or working, I feel like I am given more opportunities as an alum of such high-profile schools as Harvard and MIT. Of course, standing out is important , but success depends ons your own efforts and ability to continually grow.

If you go to Harvard, the first thing you will gain is the limitless connections made at Harvard and MIT with highly effective individuals. Personally, I think the reason why the best schools in the world are "the best" is not because of their quality of education, but rather the ambitious people who gather in one place to study and achieve great things together. In this atmosphere, you are more likely to be motivated, work harder, and grow. You will also build a web of personal connections that will help you succeed in the future.

*8. What are you currently doing now or plan on doing in the future?*

Currently, I am about to enter my third year of law school. After graduation, I am planning to work as a technical lawyer at a global law firm called Latham & Watkins. The more technology advances, the more it becomes a concern of policy makers. If you don't develop appropriate policies in coherence with newly developing technologies, it creates an array of unexpected problems in society. You need both legal and political expertise, in addition to knowledge about the complex technologies, to create effective policies to prevent them. I want to be a policy-maker who can play this role in the long term.

*Summary of Key Points:*

1. For Students: Studying is a cooperative activity. You can reinforce your understanding of certain concepts by teaching the material to a friend (or a few) in detail.
2. For Parents: Top universities are not only known for the quality of the academics, but for the personal qualities of the people that study there. If a student is surrounded by other hardworking and driven individuals, then, in turn, he or she

will receive a healthy dose of pressure to work hard and grow as an individual.

3. For law school applicants, think about cultivating other substandard knowledge that can be applied to a legal profession.

*Review:*

From attending UC Berkeley, to getting his Ph.D. at MIT, to now entering his third year at Harvard Law School, Alan has had more than his fair share of studying at some of the world's top institutions. He comes to the conclusion that learning should be done together with peers, and that knowledge should be shared as much as possible. This belief led him to start his own YouTube channel, MentorsTV, dedicated to openly sharing study tips and academic knowledge with students. His engineering background and experience working in Silicon Valley strengthened his Harvard Law School application, and compensated for his below average LSAT score (which is a crucial component for law school applications).

# The Sustainable Architect & Aspiring Professor

## Jung Min Han

**Education:**
Harvard Graduate School of Design PhD, Sustainable Architecture/Building Performance Simulation, Class of 2021 or 2022
Carnegie Mellon University, Master of Science

**Hometown:**
Seoul, South Korea

*What are your quirks? What do you think makes you unique?*

I enjoy combining two things that seem rather unrelated. For example, I would imagine what it would be like to be a piano playing athlete or a dentist who draws. In fact, I used to tell my parents that I wanted to become a poet who also does math and science.

Today, as a doctoral student at the Harvard School of Design School, I am conducting research on the topic of deep neural networks based in computer science.

*1. What kind of child were you growing up and what were your interests?*

Because my dad finished his Ph.D. in Germany, I lived there when I was very young. However, I received my elementary, middle, and high school education in Korea. Since my mother graduated from college in the U.S., and my father did his residency in the U.S., I grew up thinking that I should follow in their footsteps and study abroad, as well.

As a little kid, I naturally gravitated towards STEM subjects. I was drawn to math and science particularly because I hated being exposed to the same information repetitively, so I was always looking to experiment and learn new information. My mother had a busy schedule, so, growing up, I spent more time with my father, like doing on weekend trips. Looking back, I had a pretty happy childhood. I not only studied hard to impress my busy parents, who were doing their best to provide for the family, but also because I was just naturally competitive, striving to be the best in everything that I do.

Coming from a family of dentists, my parents wanted me to become one too. I had a lot of arguments with my parents over this, as I am sure many teenagers around the world also experience when discussing their futures with their families. The truth was, I never wanted to be a doctor. I negotiated with myself that I would at least gain acceptance to a school that they wanted me to attend, but with my SAT scores lower than expected, that was not possible. From then on, I decided that I would become the best in my chosen field to make my parents proud.

Against my parents' hopes that I would become a dentist, I attended an art school to study architecture. This choice seemed to contradict my identity as a STEM girl who loved solving math problems. Oddly, I've never painted in my life, so I had to gain admission to the school through my high math and science scores. From then on, I forged my own path, and fell in love with architecture. However, I felt that the progress I was making was limited, so I decided to study abroad to find new opportunities and broaden my horizons.

*2. How involved were your parents in helping you to prepare for Harvard? How did they help you to learn and grow?*

Thanks to my busy parents, I have developed the ability to study independently.

Unlike other Korean mothers, my mother didn't actively look for academies and private tutors to supplement my studies. I think she thought it was natural to study and learn independently. Whether this was attributed to her position as a professor or her school days spent in the U.S., she wasn't really invested in private education. Nevertheless, she was always supportive, and granted me a lot of freedom.

When I was in middle school, I attended an academy for the first time . I chose to attend this academy of my own volition.  In order to gain admittance to the academy, I took an entrance exam (for the very first time) and scored into a class that was at a suitable level for me. Afterwards, I told my mom that I wanted to attend this certain academy, and asked if she would be okay with paying for the tuition. She agreed wholeheartedly, perhaps impressed that I took the initiative to seek supplementary education. Since then, I got into the habit of doing research on my own to gather information that I needed.  Later on, when I began preparations to study abroad, there were a lot of responsibilities I had to fulfill with no guidance. I began to appreciate that my parents raised me to become an independent individual. In fact, I didn't even mention my plans to them until my acceptance to Harvard. After getting into Harvard, their happiness and support has motivated me to work even harder.

My mother also taught me a valuable lesson. She majored in music, and played the violin all her life. She later chose to pick up playing the viola. Her decision was strategic, since, back then in Korea, the viola was not as popular as the violin. As a result, there were not as many talented violists. My mother realized that, due to lack of competition, even with a little extra effort, she could rise above the rest. She often advised me, "Find areas where you can work a little bit differently to gain a competitive edge; particularly in areas that people have not yet explored or have a hard time doing. Find your niche." As I started my master's and doctorate degrees, I knew exactly how to apply this advice.

*3. What is your most memorable memory in preparation for Harvard and what was something you experienced that you never thought you ever would?*

I got my master's degree from Carnegie Mellon University. Since CMU is known for its computer science program, all master's students were required to take two computer science classes. Through these mandatory classes, I fell in love with programming. As an architect, it was challenging to take classes among engineers, but since I was a STEM girl at heart, I was able to keep up easily. Coding became my "weapon." Although my master's thesis was on mechanical engineering, I developed an optimization software run on solar panels that measured the angle of the panels. Only then did I understand my mother's advice to "find my niche." I decided to go back to design school, and applied to Harvard, highlighting this optimization software of mine in my application.

Ultimately, my dream was to receive a doctorate degree in the U.S. After completing my master's degree at CMU, I applied to doctoral programs. I was offered acceptance into a Ph.D. program at another institution, but I was also accepted into a master's program at the Harvard Graduate School of Design. I was interested in the master's program, but I hesitated due to the risk of not being able to pursue my goal of attaining a Ph.D. after a second master's degree. However, my parents gave me so much support, assuring me that it wasn't a waste of time and that it would be a good experience.

After two years in the master's degree program at the Harvard Graduate School of Design, I was lucky to receive a lot of guidance from a professor there. Today, I am currently in my third year of the doctoral program at Harvard.

*4. Study tips you have for younger students.*

First, I would like to advise those preparing to take the GRE or TOEFL that there is no need to memorize the definitions of 40,000 words. Although the vocabulary words may be useful for the test, they did not serve me on a daily basis throughout my master's and doctoral courses. I regret not using that time to buy a textbook for my intended major, and use that to study English, instead.

Unlike in Korean society, where passive personalities are preferred, the U.S. appreciates students who are actively seeking their own opportunities. In my opinion, living passively, whether it involves needlessly worrying about others' opinions or that one's own way of thinking is probably wrong, is a huge waste of opportunity. So what if a plan doesn't work out? I urge people to be confident and attempt new things, despite what anybody else thinks.

*5. What do you believe was your "X" factor to gain an admission to Harvard?*

I studied engineering, which most designers are unfamiliar with. With my engineering background, I have been using software-based tools and models to expand the scope of my specialty. I think I was able to come this far by studying the subjects most design students tend to avoid. Of course, learning about programming and engineering is nothing special at an engineering school, but at a design school, these skills are rare. For this reason, many of my colleagues, and even my professors, tend to reach out to me when they have a programming or engineering question.

While working towards both of my master's degrees, I was often doing coding work, including data organizing and design, and later developed "automated workflow" to submit to professors. I simplified the boring and repetitive design process that the school has been using by automating it.

I took this development a step further by learning about software programs that students couldn't use or didn't really understand how to use. I held workshops to teach other designers how to use such tools in a simplified way. Through these initiatives, I started to become a somewhat vital resource to the School of Design.

I knew that neither my English proficiency nor my designs could surpass my peers, so my goal was to be unique  by applying engineering to this field.   One of my professors even offered me a research assistantship due to my coding skills.

During my time as a master's student in the Harvard Graduate School of Design, I wanted to  gain the opportunity to work under the only professor who specialized in eco-friendly designs at Harvard. This was not easy. The professor was so busy that my emails would go unanswered. In some cases, student assistants would reply in his stead. Nevertheless, I still wanted to earn the favor of this professor. I hoped he would be my advisor for my master's thesis and help me pursue my doctoral studies. I must have sent more than 20 emails and prepared an hour-long presentation. The professor finally gave me a chance.

After giving my presentation, I later found out that one of his current advisee's doctoral thesis was remarkably similar. My interests coincided with those of the professor, so he happily agreed to become my advisor. From then on, we have been holding regular one-on-one meetings, which eventually led to the extension of my research. Perseverance in spite of rejection and failure allowed me to eventually find success.

*6. What are some of the challenges you have faced in school?*

There are more than 1,000 students at the Harvard Graduate School of Design. In a school as big as this, opportunities do not come to you unless you look for them yourself. Other master's programs usually have fewer students, so students receive more individual attention from professors. I had to look for opportunities like research assistantships and teaching assistantships on my own. This may be difficult for students who are shy or wait to be approached.

*7. What do you find most valuable about your Harvard education?*

Despite the stress of starting my studies at Harvard, I was so happy to be on campus because famous architects were teaching my classes and roaming the halls. I attended a number of classes taught by top architects I've long admired.

Another plus was that I could cross register with MIT, so I even ended up writing a paper with an MIT professor, as well—something I couldn't imagine myself doing. And when I realized that I wanted to gain teaching experience, I was able to find opportunities through J-term classes (classes held in January), Summer Discovery, being a teaching assistant, and even the Harvard Extension School. I'm very thankful for these endless opportunities offered here at Harvard.

*8. What are you currently doing now or plan on doing in the future?*

I think my greatest goal at the moment is to study hard until I graduate, and to produce as many papers in the time that I have left. Ultimately, I would like to become a professor.

If you are someone who is willing to create a new career, go ahead and carve out your own path. It's a seed of thought I would like to plant in students.

*Summary of Key Points:*

1.  For Students: Be persistent if there is a project, internship, or work experience you would like to pursue, whether that would be with a teacher, professor, or an expert from an industry. They may ignore all your calls and emails at first, but don't let this discourage you. If you consistently indicate interest, you may finally be given the chance you were waiting for.
2.  For Parents: Remind students to find their niche. Doing what everybody else is doing will only entail greater competition, and lower chances to stand out.
3.  Do not spend an excessive amount of time preparing for standardized tests. Better use of your time would be reading books and articles for your intended course of study. This will

allow you to come into the program well-equipped and well-versed in your major.

*Review:*

Jung Min knew that her parents had the best intentions for her when they urged her to become a dentist. But, she followed her instinct that the medical field was not right for her, and chose a career in architecture, instead. Her unique background in engineering and programming allowed her to serve as an invaluable resource in her academic community. She encourages students to  take the road less traveled, and to be a little rebellious when called for.

# The Business Woman & Fearless Explorer

## Dahye Choi

**Education:**
Harvard Business School, Master of Business Administration, Class of 2021
Yonsei University, School of Business,

**Working Experience:**
Senior Associate, BCG Seoul, Dayli Financial Group
Head of Strategy and Planning, Fintech Startup

*1. What kind of child were you growing up, and what were your interests?*

When I was a kid, I was an adapter as well as an explorer. I didn't shy away from any new experiences or chances to learn through toys, books, parks, games, books, and sports.

You can say that I had a mind of my own. I liked to enter speaking contests and debating with others and didn't have any trouble expressing what was exactly on my mind. I was frank and honest and didn't try to hide anything. Most parents let their children go on a trip on their own may be the best junior or senior year of high school. But for me, during my first year of middle school, I went on a trip on my own. I had the confidence that I could thrive in any new environment I found myself in.

I studied hard during middle and high school and was even given the "model student" title by my teachers and peers. For my undergraduate studies, I went to the Business School at Yonsei University in Seoul, South Korea. Back then, I even took the Harvard undergraduate acceptance test, which is a test to see if you will be likely to get accepted by the school and what your prominent qualities were. My results showed that my strong suits were in the arts and sports in addition to academics. However, I didn't really have time to focus on that many extracurricular activities because juggling schoolwork already proved to be a challenge for me.

*2. How involved were your parents in helping you to prepare for Harvard? How did they help you to learn and grow?*

For the MBA admission, there are not many things parents could do in terms of hands-on support. I mean, the average age of an HBS student is twenty-seven. But what I did really appreciate was the fact that my parents gave me unconditional trust in my decision, which enabled me to be more independent.

Knowing that studying abroad was an entirely new endeavor, my parents easily could have said, 'It's too dangerous. Don't do it," or "You don't know about studying or living abroad," or even, I'm really worried about you. Moving to a new country sounds risky. Let me help you as much as possible." They basically gave me the freedom to do whatever I wanted to do. Over time, their trust allowed me to set goals and make decisions independently in the long run.

Although this may seem like a small thing for many people, I am also really grateful to them for developing my reading habit. We didn't own a television when I was young. This may actually sound awful for many people out there as to how I even survived childhood without television, but it gave me a lot of time to read books and fall in love with reading. It's an important life skill that has served me well for many years, both in my personal and academic life. Also, because of their emphasis on reading, listening, and talking to one another, I was able to fine tune my comprehension skills from a young age.

*3. What is your most memorable memory in preparation for Harvard, and what was something you experienced that you never thought you ever would?*

I joined the Boston Consulting Group after graduating from college. I decided to apply for a consulting firm because I thought it was a place where I could gain a lot of experience by being exposed to various stakeholders, geographic regions, and industries. Looking back even now, I think it was the right decision. I learned what a good presentation and what a good analysis looked like through working at BCG.

Additionally, all of my colleagues that I have met during my time working at the consulting firm are still really great friends of mine. Working amongst a group of smart and passionate people had a positive impact on me. There were a lot of business trips and even a chance to work at the Tokyo office. Due to these opportunities, I've been able to broaden my outlook on the world.

After that, I moved to Fintech, but if I had to work as an advisor to the consulting company, I thought that I might as well for myself. I was also working in a dynamic industry that was rapidly emerging at the time. In consulting, you usually only interact with people with expertise in your field. However, at Fintech, I learned how to collaborate with people from entirely different backgrounds, including engineers and designers. Also, if reports and analyses are the majority of work at other consulting companies, at Fintech, you were expected to do everything aside from development and design, so I was able to do a variety of tasks myself.

Even after I decided to study abroad, the process of preparing for an MBA was really hard for me. I didn't want rumors to circulate at work that I was trying to apply for an MBA application while still showing up to work to receive a paycheck. I found it difficult to squeeze in time even on the weekends after work to spend time on my application—from the GMAT to getting letters of recommendation, and writing admissions essays. There never seemed to be enough time. But I also could not complain to anyone as this was a task I had put upon myself to achieve.

For Harvard's MBA application, I remember the essays had prompts focused on seeing a holistic view of one's life. They asked questions that examined my decision-making process and the obstacles I've overcome. These questions were probably the most difficult for me. I've never practiced asking myself these questions daily, so it forced me to self-reflect over the past thirty years of my life.

*4. Study tips you have for younger students.*

Many students work hard and aspire to get into Harvard. Still, many students and applicants have to realize that Harvard might not be the greatest fit for your academic and career goals and will not guarantee that your life will be stellar after you graduate. Making the most out of the surrounding resources is what opens up new opportunities. In my case, my hard work at BCG paid off, and I was able to work abroad. Additionally, because I was good at my job, I received the "fun" projects that everyone wanted, outstanding recommendation letters, and help from my colleagues and seniors.

Likewise, I think it is essential to identify your personal reason as to why you want to work hard. I think the key is to find a place where you can give value to what you pursue. In my case, I love new things. As a person who enjoys learning new things, doing new things, and trying out the latest trends, I just happened to end up at a consulting firm. Then, I happened to go to Fintech, where there is always a new project waiting in store for me. It is exciting for me to be in this ever-changing creative environment.

On the other hand, if my job was one that asked for consistency and patience, I might not have done well or worked as hard. I knew I couldn't commit myself to ten years of studying, so I didn't pursue a Ph.D. although I commend those who have the diligence and passion to do so. However, I was able to find an environment where I could keep trying new things. I think I was able to find my path through the process of elimination after sifting through my likes, dislikes, and strengths.

Lastly, I think surrounding yourself with many hardworking friends, and colleagues plays a key factor in your success. I find myself feeling guilty when I'm next to people who are working hard, and I'm not. When you start spending time with people you think are cool and accomplished, I believe their standards naturally begin to rub off on you.

*5. What do you believe was your "X" factor to gain admission to Harvard?*

I think my "X" factor was my contribution to creativity and new technology in my company's transformation.

Working at BCG and Fintech, I carried out many projects upgrading companies through new technology or management methods, specifically by introducing technology in finance. I think these qualities help me stand out through my resume and my SOP (statement of Purpose).

I tried to make the Harvard admissions officers think somewhat along the lines, "Hey, this is a kid that can easily adapt to new environments, and even after he graduates from Harvard will face challenges head-on rather than running away from them."

Compared to other business schools, Harvard requires at least 2-3 years of working experience, but usually, 4-5 years or more is the standard. That is why the average age of students here is about twenty-eight. Thus, scholars with some work experience gather from all over the world at Harvard Business School to study business administration for two years. It's really exciting to meet this many experienced and talented individuals all in one place. You just learn so much from each other. If you graduate here, most will go back and do business. Another factor that differentiates Harvard from other schools is that they don't teach out of textbooks, and instead, focus on taking a deep dive case-by-case and through presentations. HBS divides students up by sections and assigns designated seats. This seat is my spot for the rest of the semester. The professor has the role of an orchestra conductor, but because he can't teach the entire content in a certain period, most of it is self-taught by myself and my friends. We are given the same cases, but we still end up with conflicting perspectives. The insight achieved through such methods is what I like to call the "Harvard Way."

For these reasons, it is important who you are studying with and where their level of participation lies. The atmosphere here where everyone is actively participating and raising their hands with questions and answers is something not found in other schools. Regular "lectures" do not seem to exist in this university.

*6. What are some challenges you have faced in school?*

The classes themselves are difficult.

Firstly, it is hard to digest all the reading within the given time. Also, since I'm not a native speaker, there were a lot of obstacles for me to read a new case every night at the level of a native English-speaker. I am also expected to form my own opinions on the given content. There are various subjects in the management school (accounting, strategy, marketing, technology) that I'm not that good at, so it's hard to form my own opinions and express them in front of more than 100 students. I was hesitant and even scared to make comments that might make me look stupid or not be able to come up with a sufficient rebuttal if someone doesn't agree with my opinion. I was able to overcome these fears by having a mindset that, "If I don't know, then they don't know either. I tell myself that the reason why Harvard chose me is because of my different background; I should have confidence because I will contribute to their experience. This environment is something we all are not used to, so it's also a matter of language that makes it difficult. This challenge applies to all students regardless of what your first language is or where you are from.

Additionally, there are too many conferences, social events, mixers, travel classes, events, recruiting, coffee dates, etc. It's impossible to attend them all. That is why you constantly feel FOMO (fear of missing out) here. That is why you have to know why and what specifically you want to accomplish here at Harvard to be able to escape these feelings of missing out on the social aspect of attending a university. It was personally challenging for me to overcome my FOMO and manage my schedule.

*7. What do you find most valuable about your Harvard education?*

I really like the school environment because there is enough space and opportunities to make mistakes to learn and grow. At work, errors can be fatal, but a school is a place for you to learn and the professors and teaching staff are all there to help you out.

I need to do my best, but I think it's better to experiment a lot in the opportunities presented to me. Making mistakes is okay. For example, if you have a school presentation and want to try presenting it differently, you are given a chance to experiment.

I see every student sitting around me in class just as my professors and view us all in one sitting. Learning not only comes in the form of professors but also through class discussions with fellow students. I like the fact that I get to interact with various people from different cultural, social, academic, and career backgrounds who share their opinions actively. Their existence alone makes this school special.

Of course, some kids are naturally smart, but some people have experienced hardship, overcame them, and have surprising knowledge in certain areas. I think it's amazing that I'm always surrounded by extremely smart people in their respective fields and passions.

*8. What are you currently doing now or plan on doing in the future?*

I'm the type to do my very best at every given moment, so rather than having a grand long-term plan or vision, I just know that I would like to work in the business area that utilizes technology for a long time. I think my path will become more apparent if I continue to work hard as I do now.

*Summary of Key Points:*

1. For Students: If you are interested in applying to Harvard Business School, it is best to have two to three years of working experience under your belt before you decide to pursue an MBA. Having four to five years of experience is even better.
2. For Parents: Engage your children in constant conversation and debates at home so that they develop the confidence to speak up for themselves in various settings.
3. Surround yourself with friends and peers who are high-achievers and passionate about what they do, and you will find that their energy and drive will rub on you as well.

*Review:*

From a young age, Dahye knew the meaning of making the most of every experience and opportunity. Instead of whining to her parents why she could not watch television like the rest of her childhood friends, she used the screen time she would have had to delve into reading books instead. Dahye highly credits her parents for giving her the confidence to become an independent person and giving her life tools such as her critical thinking skills and her passion for reading. She emphasizes the need for experience in the world and your respective field to come into graduate programs prepared and ready to engage with the rest of your peers.

# The Business Analyst & (Almost Professional Athlete)

## Dylan Kim

**Education:**
Harvard Business School, General Management, Class of 2019
Sogang University, BA in Business Administration, Class of 2007 cum laude

**Working Experience:**
Business Analyst, Samsung C&T Management Group
Platoon Commander First Lieutenant, Republic of Korea 17th Division Officer

**Hometown:**
Seoul, South Korea

*What are your quirks? What do you think makes you unique?*

I love to exercise. Nearly until the end of middle school, I wanted to become a professional athlete, so I would exercise a lot. Though I ended up heading towards the academic route, I continued to work out. I also played football when I got to college.

*1. What kind of child were you growing up, and what were your interests?*

A typical comment left throughout my school records was that I 'daydreamed a lot.' I grew up as a child who liked to imagine and think. Actually, I don't think I studied that hard. I just wanted to go out and play, so I would try to finish my studies quickly. Still, I tried to follow my parents' wishes, so I had to finish my studies as fast as possible to have fun. I spent my childhood doing things quickly.

I didn't study hard, but I wanted to go to a particular high school with my friends, so I got determined to take the test. Eventually, I got into Daewon Foreign Language school with two other people from my school. A lot of people were curious about how I got in because I was just a child that loved sports.

Looking back on my high school years, I didn't particularly get into a college as highly ranked as what most kids from my school usually go to. But I didn't want to take a year off to retake the exam.

I went along with the curriculum set up by the Korean education system throughout my youth. But once I got into college, I loved the fact that we got to choose our own classes. Management was an interesting subject, but I think business was a subject that matched my interests so well that some people refused to call it academic. Until after I entered Sogang University, I began studying like a junior in high school, reading books all day at the library. After returning from my military service as an officer, I decided to think about my career. There was a law school system in Korea at that time, and I thought it might be fun to go to law school. I took the LEET test and luckily got an excellent score. I did so well that I could pick almost any law school of my liking.

At the same time, I was also preparing to secure a job at a company. I had to choose which career path to take: law or business. I didn't think I'd be happy with my life as a lawyer. Rather than spending a life defending clients and sinners, I preferred a management and business path where I would get to travel the world and a lifestyle that would bring me happiness. My decision to give up on law school was also my choice to join Samsung.

*2. How involved were your parents in helping you to prepare for Harvard? How did they help you to learn and grow?*

My parents raised me differently because they knew that I was different from my brother. My brother always graduated from first in school and was one of the top five in Korea. But when you take individual exams, you can sometimes get beat out by someone else- say he lost his valedictorian spot and got second- no matter how excellent his grades were, my mother would often chastise my brother a lot. My mother, who saw through his ability and personality, knew that he would be better off if she was stricter and controlling like a Tiger Mom. My brother continually did well academically and eventually got accepted to Seoul National University.

On the other hand, I would only study enough to rank second in my classroom and 20th in the class, yet my mother would never get mad at me. When we talked about these years later and that it was because my mother realized that if she treated me like how she did to my brother, it was clear that I would act out.

My parents let me do whatever I wanted to do at a young age. As long as it wasn't illegal or impolite, they allowed me to do many things with no restrictions. When I was little, I would say that I wanted to become a soccer player, and in middle school, I suddenly announced that I wanted to become a basketball player. They didn't oppose either time. Looking back now, I can see that it was clearly too late for me to become an elite athlete and not physically fit enough. My mother was probably strongly opposed to it in her mind, but she allowed me to go ahead to meet the national team and coaches for a test anyway.

Growing up in such an environment, I developed a personality that refused to shy away from new or difficult situations. I learned to make decisions based on my judgment through the hands-on experience without fear of challenges. Naturally, I lost my unwillingness to challenge new things.

My father also instilled the confidence that I'll get into Harvard from a young age. He had a habit of saying, "You're going to Harvard." It all came back after I got my job and was preparing to apply for an MBA. I started to think about it again. Eventually, his words came true over the years for both my brother and me.

Thanks to my wise parents, I was able to develop well. They definitely played a critical role in my HBS admission.

*3. What is your most memorable memory in preparation for Harvard, and what was something you experienced that you never thought you ever would?*

Students who come to Harvard MBA are usually coming in after working very hard in their careers, so they don't have time to reflect on their lives. The truth is that you need to unpack and organize your career history to apply for an MBA. This is very important, in fact. I, too, had very little time to take a step back and reflect.

As my experiences were compiled together and form my traits, they became a foundation for my career; Everything seemed to unfold like a story. It felt refreshing to have this time to reflect on myself and made it really easy to write an essay afterward.

After I decided to go for an MBA, I applied for the Samsung sponsorship program for my MBA. I was one of the 20 chosen out of the 200,000 employees that year. I think I was selected because the company thought that this investment would bring about a greater output in the long run.

*4. Study tips you have for younger students.*

Firstly, it is most important to find the reason and purpose to study on your own. Don't do it just when someone tells you to. Find the reason why you want to learn it because once you become curious about a specific subject and field, learning becomes more fun and easy. And study hard. The amount of studying you're doing right now may seem useless right now, but it will become helpful for any part of your life. There is no such thing as studying that is "meaningless."

I would also like to emphasize concentration. Korean students tend to study hard for 18 hours in one place, but there are limits to our concentration. If someone can only concentrate for four hours when they study, they will still only study for four even if they sit for eight hours. The remaining four hours then wouldn't actually be time spent studying. That's why I'd like to advise students not to be tied up to the concept of studying with a strict time frame. Only sit down to learn when you can use 100% of your focus.

Instead, I'd take a break at that time to take a break, sleep, exercise, or watch TV. Then when I think my concentration is back, I go back to study. I think this method is the most efficient method of learning. Sitting down in one place for 8-10 hours at a time will most likely tire you out.

It's good to practice this skill. When I was young, I liked to play outside, but I also enjoyed reading books. My parents loved to read, and so did my brother. Naturally, I grew to love books too. There were many books at home, and I enjoyed rereading books. Slowly, my concentration developed, and as I grew older, I could concentrate longer.

I want to tell every student to please exercise, no matter how busy you are with your studies. You have to maintain good physical health to help keep your brain healthy as well. Studying is a very strenuous activity, after all.

*5. What do you believe was your "X" factor to gain admission to Harvard?*

Harvard MBA admissions officers make it very clear what students they want. The Harvard Business School is like a machine that picks people to make a difference in society. They choose those specific people to educate, eventually creating people who will change society and the world.

That is why I was chosen because my life experiences and achievements at work matched the standards that Harvard was looking for.

Even though I wasn't in a high position and may make some people uncomfortable, I choose to speak out and find solutions. I would say, "We have to make a change," and persuaded my higher-ups to make the change. I tried to convey my leadership and communication skills well in this way. That's why I think Harvard chose me.

*6. What are some challenges you have faced in school?*

Everything was difficult at first. I went to a foreign language high school, and I didn't find it hard to have a casual conversation. However, this was my first time studying everything in English. To add to that, attending a school like Harvard that attracts students from all over the world meant that I had to learn to understand all their accents and words. Also, I had to explain and learn in English that everyone could understand, which was very difficult for me. I got used to it after the first semester, but English was definitely a big challenge.

Harvard MBA was completely different from the Korean teaching method. Here, everything is taught through what is called a 'case method.' There would be a person typing down every presentation and comment the students would make in class, which would then be collected by the professor at the end of class. From then, they would grade you accordingly to the comments said. This database would be combined with the term essay for your final score. With this data, the professor would purposely give cold calls on students that were not participating as much in class. They give them out at the beginning or during lectures so no one would know when they would get called on. It created an environment where you had to be ready to make presentations constantly.

I was going to every class and doing well, but suddenly, the professor called on me to make a presentation. This concept was hard to understand at first. I was expected to raise my hand whenever I wanted to speak, and when I was picked, 90 faces would turn around and stare at me.

However, two years of repeating this, I now realize that there is no better teaching method. If you don't prepare beforehand, it's impossible to keep up, so it is practically mandatory.

*7. What do you find most valuable about your Harvard education?*

Based on my experience, I really liked the part when I would talk about things that other people had not experienced, getting sympathy from each other, and sharing opinions. This is a hard topic to bring up in Korean lecture culture, so this was an extremely valuable experience to have.

Also, Harvard MBA students who all have had busy lives up until this moment, use this as a chance to travel everywhere. There were many instances where people leave to travel abroad on Friday and come back Sunday evening. That's why I traveled a lot as well. There was also an opportunity connected to the school where I could go abroad to Greece and work with a company, making many good memories.

*8. What are you doing now or plan on doing in the future?*

Currently, I'm working at Samsung. What I'm doing right now is setting standards for allocating management resources so that the company's strategy can be realized, creating systems and tasks to help the company strengthen its capabilities and use them.

After graduation, I started a big project as soon as I got back to the company because of the high expectations given to a Harvard alum. I started a project to create a whole new framework for the company, and now I'm busy having fun with the follow-up project.

Actually, a lot of people from my company ask me a lot of questions like this. They ask, "Why did you come back to the same company and not try other things or find a job in the US?" The fact is, I really enjoy what I do in this company. And when I came back, they gave me work that was even more fun. Of course, these are challenging times, but since they keep giving me enjoyable work, I have fallen in love with my work.

*Summary of Key Points:*

1. For Students: The Harvard Business School is looking for leadership qualities in their applicants. People who are not afraid to stand up for what they believe in, even if it means going against popular opinion or traditions. Think about what kind of leader you are, would like to be, and how to portray yourself as in your applications.

2. For Parents: Your child may have a grand dream to pursue a particular career path even though you believe he or she may not eventually follow that path. It is best to offer the resources and support to the child to show initiative that you believe in their abilities.

3. The high school or undergraduate university you have gone through maybe have a reputation for sending their students to certain schools in higher education. It is easy to compare yourself to your peers if you do not end up at these "expected" schools. What's more important is to focus on what you are interested in studying and finding your passion, your niche, your unique angle within your intended field of study.

*Review:*

In comparison to his older brother, Dylan was raised with a different set of expectations from his parents and experienced a more hands-off approach. So, instead of using the time to worry about his class rank, he utilized the time to search for experiences. This would help him advance his interests in business and management and help him experiment in what he wanted to do in the future—including his childhood pursuits of becoming a professional athlete at one point in time. He urges students not just to study because someone has told you to, but to learn when you find personal reasons. Everything else will fall in place.

# The Computational Designer & Automator

## Joonhaeng Lee

**Education:**
Harvard Graduate School of Design, Master of Design Studies in Technology, Class of 2021
Yonsei University, Bachelor of Architecture, Major, Class of 2016

**GPA and Test Scores:**
Yonsei University GPA, (3.4/4.3)

**Extracurriculars and Awards:**
National Science & Technology Scholarship
*Full scholarship as a student excellence in mathematics and science.*

**Working Experience:**
Building Information Modeling (BIM) Consultant, Syntegrate, 3 Years
*Participated in six building façade projects in Korea and Japan.*

**Hometown:**
Seoul, South Korea

*What are your quirks? What do you think makes you unique?*

A lot of my friends would say that I'm nerdy. As for a "quirk," I would say I'm quite gifted at logically breaking down real-life problems into math or science problems, and solving them. For example, whenever I see an ordinary task in my daily life, I get an urge to find the optimal solution by automating and programming the task. I feel like I'm slowly becoming a robot.

*1. What kind of child were you growing up and what were your interests?*

As a child, I liked using my hands to create 3D objects. I would take different pieces of furniture around my house, such as desks, tables, and chairs, to stack up and build high structures with. Throughout my elementary and middle school years, I would play with Legos and assemble play models every day. Whenever I came across issues I couldn't solve, I was a stubborn child that would refuse to eat or sleep until it had all been solved. During high school, in my car and airplane research class, I learned how to cut iron, glass, and put together cars.

For me, the process of creating a desired form out of materials and objects is very similar to math and science. I loved both subjects immensely,and received a full scholarship to Yonsei University's Architecture program.

Even today, at Harvard, I am still using math to make sculptures. Though I have come a long way since my childhood years of tinkering with Legos and stacking pieces of furniture on top of one another, I think the basic principles are still all there.

*2. How involved were your parents in helping you to prepare for Harvard? How did they help you to learn and grow?*

Both of my parents were born and raised in the countryside. They moved to Seoul for college and lived sophisticated and comfortable lives. Neither had any experience with studying abroad in the U.S., and never pushed me to go to Harvard or to go study abroad at all. However, I grew up respecting my parents' way of life, which later encouraged me to apply to Harvard.

My mother, who was a high school teacher, liked to read and study at home in her spare time. There were always a lot of worn books next to my mother. So, naturally, I would also carry around my own collection of favorite books to read. My father, who was always busy working at a large company, was a very dedicated family man. During my school years, he would cook a lot of delicious meals, and talk about the economy, society, and history for hours on the weekends. Both of my parents do not watch TV, but love to read, instead. Growing up, I think watching their incredible work ethic influenced me to become the same kind of individual.

Neither of my parents interfered with my career path and interests. They always supported me, no matter what. This supportive environment allowed me to take the initiative in establishing my desired career path.

*3. What is your most memorable memory in preparation for Harvard and what was something you experienced that you never thought you ever would?*

I was working at the time I applied. The work itself was fun and important, so I couldn't afford to spend any of my working hours on my application.

I spent a year working on the application. Every morning before the start of the workday, I would go to the Starbucks across the street from my workplace in order to study. I would get there before 6:50 a.m. and stay there until 10 a.m. When I got off work, I would go to the library, and then be back at the Starbucks until midnight. I continued this routine of studying for five to six hours a day for a year. How you performed on the test is important, and sometimes, there isn't any time to self-reflect at all. If you are considering applying to graduate schools, I recommend that you constantly ask yourself, "Who am I? What am I? What do I want to do in the future?" This will save you time and allow you to submit a quality application. I did a lot of self-reflecting in the year I spent working on the application. Over a period of six months, I carried around my statement of purpose (SOP) printed on an A4-sized paper. I took the SOP everywhere I went, and edited the paper every chance I had, whether it be jotting down a new idea or revising my words.

*4. Study tips you have for younger students.*

In my case, I finished undergrad in Korea and came to the U.S. for graduate school. I think undergraduate and graduate schools are two very different application experiences. When applying to grad school, you apply to study a specific field. So, for me, I personally found it easier preparing for grad school because I only had to focus on my favorite subjects. Even when I was preparing my portfolio, it was fun because I got to choose what projects to work on. In contrast, when I was applying to colleges, I would often ask myself in frustration why I had to study certain subjects. Preparing for grad school is the time for students to sharpen their favorite tools in their toolkit. It's a lot more enjoyable and less stressful.

Also, at GRE prep academies, people tell you that you need to get at least a certain score in order to secure a spot at an Ivy League school. If you score a few points less, you are told that it's basically pointless to apply. Don't believe this. It is completely false.

I didn't find much of a difference between studying at Yonsei and at Harvard, although the benefit of attending a top school like Harvard did expose me to more outstanding students and well-known professors. The amount of work and difficulty of classes was mostly the same. In the case of high schools in Korea, students spend most of their time learning how to be great test-takers. At the end of the day, the sole focus is what score they received, without having a single clue on what they would like to do for the rest of their lives. Eventually, academics becomes an extremely stressful experience, instead of an opportunity to discover your interests. It's just sad.

*5. What do you believe was your "X" factor to gain an admission to Harvard?*

It was very important for me to put together a portfolio that would show who I was—not only as a designer, but as an individual. I had three years of work experience at an architectural consulting firm that showcased my personal interest and professional pursuits. I was able to compile my work at the firm, and create a distinctive portfolio. I traveled to and from Korea, Japan and Hong Kong to participate in six different building projects. It is quite rare for a person in the architecture field to have the opportunity to be in building projects. These were all amazing experiences that I was very fortunate to be a part of.

All six of the buildings were very difficult to construct, and were works designed by renowned architects. In other words, they were not simply rectangular buildings, but oddly shaped with a lot of curves. After graduating from college, I studied computer engineering on my own. I applied this knowledge to my work, which helped me create a more unique portfolio. This was my advantage in my application. There weren't that many design applicants with a programming and engineering background. Lastly, I submitted a portfolio where I carefully selected my favorite design works, instead of including every single project I've ever worked on. I believe this discretion also played a big role in my acceptance to Harvard.

*6. What are some of the challenges you have faced in school?*

During my undergraduate years, I think every opportunity was pretty much openly announced to everyone. However, at Harvard, a lot of opportunities and valuable information were given by professors to their favorite students under-the-table or exchanged between close friends. For instance, in the beginning, I wasn't really paying attention to the conversations that were going on, but, one day, I found my friend working at a lab that I was not aware of. These opportunities and information came through email or were posted on the bulletin board, so you had to remain alert at all times—a concept that I had to get used to at first. That is why I purposely attended casual events, parties, or informal meetings to get information. I would then send an email to the professor, "I just heard about this opportunity passing by and I have the skills for this…" These cultural differences, and having to learn how to reach out first was my greatest challenge when it came to adjusting to an American university.

*7. What do you find most valuable about your Harvard education?*

My program, Master of Design Studies, serves as an example of how students can make their own career path. There are only one or two subjects that are strictly required. This flexibility can be both an advantage and a disadvantage. As someone who is personally interested in origami, I take specific programming or computerizing classes for origami. I think a big advantage of this program is that each of us has a personalized curriculum that allows us to develop and explore these interests in depth. Also, I get excited to meet nerds like me who are extremely passionate about what they do. Back in Korea, for some reason, I couldn't find many people with similar interests as me. But once I came to Harvard, I was able to find "my people," and that was really reassuring for me. One of the great advantages of studying and being a student at Harvard is that the people here are so humble, but so insanely outstanding.

Lastly, I really like the fact that we get to interact with world-famous professors within a meter's distance and act like it's nothing. It feels unreal when a professor you've always looked up to is sitting right in front of your eyes and you get to talk one-on-one with this person. Every day, you get to interact with a celebrity from the academic world, and you feel incredibly lucky to have that opportunity.

*8. What are you currently doing now or plan on doing in the future?*

With only one more year left, I've been thinking a lot about studying more here in Cambridge, where the intellectual environment is amazing. In the future, I would also like to create a company that develops solutions and machinery that can help designers and makers.

Now that I'll be applying for a Ph.D. program, the end feels so far. I have just started preparing. Everything is still uncertain due to the pandemic, but I am currently planning to take classes online for the upcoming semester.

*Summary of Key Points:*

1. For Students: Start writing your statement of purpose (SOP) as early as possible, and do a lot of self-reflection. Carry a copy of your SOP around with you so that you can edit it when you have the chance.

2. For Parents: Help your children discover their competitive edge when it comes to pursuing their passions. In Joonhaeng's case, his advantage was his self-taught knowledge of programming and engineering in the world of design.

3. Once in school, be proactive in seeking out opportunities for work and academic experiences through professors, the career center, and the school network. Nothing will be handed to you

*Review:*

Joonhaeng credits his work ethic to his parents,and proves that applying to graduate programs while having a full-time job is possible. He worked on his applications before and after work during designated time blocks for a whole year, even if it meant sacrificing a few hours worth of sleep each day. He brings to light that applying for graduate schools is a different animal in comparison to applying for undergraduate institutions. For Joonhaeng, it was more enjoyable to apply for graduate schools because he only had to focus on showcasing his specialty and passion, architectural design, while for undergraduate applications, there were many factors to consider and evaluate.

# The Instructional Designer & Coffee Lover

## Annie Nam

**Education:**
Harvard Graduate School of Education, Technology in Education, Class of 2020
UCLA, Business Economics and Communication Studies, Graduated in 10 Quarters/3 years

**Extracurriculars and Awards:**
Books Written:
*Education and Climate Change.* Springer Nature. (Expected 2020) Written in conjunction with Professor Fernando Reimers, Ford Foundation Professor of the Practice of International Education at the Harvard Graduate School of Education.

*Bringing English Education into the Home: A 10 Year Guide.* Seoul: Chekjji, 2019. Print.

Best-selling author on early bilingual education with practical benefits of reducing annual individual household spending of $30K+ on child's English immersion programs.

Contributed to:
*Unspoken Rules*
A book published by the Harvard Business Review Press.

**Working Experience:**
Instructional Designer, MIT Sloan School of Business, Current
Instructional Designer, Berkeley Haas School of Business, Current
Director, Top Daechi Private Schools and Academies
PR Consulting Group
Hackers Academia
International School

**Hometown:** South Korea/Japan/United States

*What are your quirks? What do you think makes you unique?*

I drink 4 to 5 cups of coffee a day. The amount of coffee in my system seems to parallel my productivity.

*1. What kind of child were you growing up and what were your interests?*

Growing up, my dad's job and his interest in real estate as an investment asset had us moving around every three years, living in over six cities in three different countries. I had to adapt quickly to my surroundings, even if it meant picking up a new language and assimilating to a new culture all within a period of a few months.

Up until the 5th grade, I wanted to be a teacher and an artist. I remember sitting my sister and younger cousins down and giving them "lectures." I asked them to copy down what I wrote on a small, make-believe chalkboard and graded their work. School was a place I truly felt at home, and I hated summer vacations because it meant I would have to go three months without getting to be in the classroom with teachers and friends I adored.

Culture, language, and schools were my main interests growing up. After graduating from an international school in Tokyo, Japan, I ended up majoring in Business Economics and Communication Studies at UCLA.

*2. How involved were your parents in helping you to prepare for Harvard? How did they help you to learn and grow?*

Looking back, my parents played a large part in influencing my career path, whether they had intended to do so or not. My mom was a homemaker and my dad had a position in finance working for a South Korean conglomerate. Both of my parents worked hard and put family first. I wanted to be like my parents: business savvy and financially literate like dad, but, simultaneously, warm and good with children like my mom.

When it came time to find jobs, I did not have a clear idea of what I wanted to do with my undergraduate degree. I found myself really wanting to teach, since I saw a lot of my friends going to Asia to teach for a year or two. My parents did not approve at first, since they didn't really see education as a "practical" major, but I pursued it anyway because it was something I really wanted to do. During college, I volunteered at a middle school in downtown Los Angeles, tutoring and mentoring inner city youth. I also had tutored throughout both high school and college and received positive feedback from parents and students. I didn't have the official "credentials" to teach back then, but I just knew I would be good at it.

I stayed in Asia for way longer than a couple of years, and I really climbed my way up in the private education sphere. I ended up as a director overseeing more than 10 teachers and several support staff for a well-known private education institution in Daechi, the neighborhood within Seoul famously known for education culture. In fact, by working for multiple private and international schools in Korea, I was actually putting to good use a lot of the finance savvy, sharp business instincts I've learnt from dad and the patient, nurturing skills I've gained from my mom. Above all else, my parents were my biggest role models in showing me how to have respect for others, work hard, and stay humble.

When I decided to apply to Harvard, my parents were my biggest cheerleaders. They were living in Tokyo while I was working in Seoul, and I'd count the days until I could fly in to Japan to see my parents to give them updates, and bounce ideas and strategies off of them on how to navigate my career and life choices.

*3. What is your most memorable memory in preparation for Harvard and what was something you experienced that you never thought you ever would?*

While I was happy to attend UCLA as an undergraduate, I had always wondered what the top students had done to get into the elite schools. It had seemed like a world far removed from mine back in high school.

Teaching hyper competitive kids in Daechi helped me understand what the most successful students do to differentiate themselves. They were eager, active, and did way more than I could have ever expected. But more than that, they actually enjoyed it. I learned so much from the students—it was like they were teaching me. I began to see that colleges wanted more than just a perfect GPA: they wanted to see the leadership, personality, and passion behind an application.

I applied to graduate schools with a different perspective from the one I had when I applied to undergraduate schools. I was very sure of who I was, what I wanted to study, what I wanted to get out of the experience, and very certain of my chances of getting in. I was working six days a week as director, wrote a book on English education in my free time, and was simultaneously putting together my graduate school applications. But none of it was a chore. I truly loved what I was doing, and drafting an application meant I got to imagine a life bigger, better, and fuller than I had now.

I had gotten into all six schools I had applied to, and received several large scholarships from some including Stanford, UPenn, and Columbia. It came down to Stanford and Harvard. One could argue that Stanford accepted fewer students into the department, which made it the more competitive program, but I knew all along it was Harvard or nothing.

*4. Study tips you have for younger students*

I'd advise students to live their lives to the fullest.

Looking back, I think it really comes down to pursuing what you love in the smartest way possible. Not everyone needs to be a software developer or work in investment banking. Everyone has a special skill or talent that can be leveraged to become his or her distinct competitive advantage.

I think finding that skill and being smart about understanding the resources and opportunities around you(not to mention putting in concrete hours of work)will truly open up a lot of doors you wouldn't have expected otherwise.

*5. What do you believe was your "X" factor to gain an admission to Harvard?*

At the core, I think it was my dedication to the field of education and my work ethic.

However, there was also a lot of strategy involved. I figured out how to apply to schools in the "right way." I researched programs and schools, and looked up the stats of those accepted on forums and even on the school website to get an understanding of who got in and who didn't. I mapped out my accomplishments and presented them in a way that allowed my application to shine. I thought ahead a year and outlined what I wanted to accomplish during my time at Harvard. I carefully chose the right recommenders. I prepared for the GRE on my own, memorizing the 3,000+ GRE vocabulary required of students while commuting to work. I also revised my statement of purpose over twenty times, getting feedback each time from peers and seniors.

As an international student, you have to provide evidence of sufficient funds for the duration of your studies. I worked for seven to eight years prior to HGSE to be able to support myself throughout the program and beyond. It was important to me that I didn't burden my parents financially with my decision to enroll in a graduate program.

*6. What are some of the challenges you have faced in school?*

At Harvard, you are surrounded by smart, ambitious students. Even when you give it your all, you feel that your output is mediocre, at best, compared to the work produced by your talented peers. In addition, with so much to do on campus in such a limited time span, you never quite completely feel satisfied, knowing you could have done more or done better.

But, some of the best lessons I've learned come as a direct result of my time on campus and  not by comparing my own progress with the progress of others—we are all on our own timelines and paths. I also reminded myself to have enough space and time to feel comfortable and satisfied with where I am headed.

Another important lesson I've learned was to speak up and stand up for myself. If I couldn't be the advocate for my needs, no one else would be.

So, in hindsight, overcoming hardships was, in fact, about building up self-confidence, setting up healthy boundaries, and being my own best friend.

## 7. What do you find most valuable about your Harvard education?

Being surrounded by a group of students who shared similar levels of passions and ambitions was an incredible experience for me. I was inspired by peers with impressive work ethic on a daily basis. Working and collaborating at 10 p.m. at night or over Sunday mornings was the norm at Harvard. I appreciated the amount of energy and passion students brought into their work.

I was also grateful for all the opportunities that Harvard afforded me. I got to write a book with a Harvard professor, worked on a project with the Harvard Business Review Press, organized numerous conferences and banquets, saw Nobel laureates in person, and met CEOs of major organizations and heads of international development agencies. This kind of exposure to the people at the top of their fields is unheard of anywhere else, and I'm so fortunate to have experienced it.

I also appreciated that students at the School of Education go off and have stellar career paths. I've seen multiple alumni working at international development agencies like the World Bank, OECD, or UNICEF. I've also seen alums in EdTech go off and work at organizations like Google, Microsoft, and McKinsey. While people may scoff at the idea of education being a "soft" field with little career potential, this was definitely not the case at HGSE (Harvard Graduate School of Education).

## 8. What are you currently doing now or plan on doing in the future?

I'm currently working on education technology projects as a staff member for MIT Sloan School of Management. I also work part time for UC Berkeley Haas School of Business. The pandemic has allowed me to work remotely for two places at once.

During these uncertain times, it's even more uncertain where life will take me, even to look ahead a couple of months in time. But I hope to continue to work hard, leverage opportunities, and find a happy balance of life and work.

*Summary of Key Points:*

1. Parents may initially be against a certain career path for their children, but it is important to have discussions as a family to know the reasons and experiences of why their children have chosen a particular path for themselves.
2. This is often an overlooked topic, but being financially independent and prepared before applying to graduate schools should be highly considered, even if it means taking several years to save money beforehand.
3. Put in the time to thoroughly research the universities and programs that seem the best fit for your personal, academic, and professional needs.

*Review:*

Annie reminds us that having a set plan and strategy to get into a certain university does work in the applicant's favor. In addition, having a community to help you with your applications, even if it is just asking friends to look over your statement of purpose, will only improve your chances even more. Some students apply for graduate schools directly upon graduation from their undergraduate institution, while others, such as Annie, build up experience first to fully utilize all aspects of graduate school. Her years of dedication to students and to the field of education helped her stand out from her peers.

# The Biostatistician & Human Rights Activist

## David Hong

**Education:**
Harvard T.H. Chan School of Public Health, MA Biostatistics, Class of 2021
Cornell University, BA Policy Analysis and Management
International School in Hong Kong, Valedictorian

**Extracurriculars and Awards:**
Dean's List for 5 semesters at Cornell, highest AMC (American Mathematics Competition) 10 score in Southeast Asia.

**Working Experience:**
I interned at Weill Cornell Medicine, Memorial Sloan Kettering Cancer Center, and Asan Medical Center in Seoul for my sophomore, junior, and after graduation summer, respectively as data analyst intern. In Memorial Sloan Kettering Cancer Center, I led and conducted a study on the relationship of publicly available hospital rankings and long-term cancer outcomes.

**Hometown:**
Hong Kong/Seoul

*What are your quirks? What do you think makes you unique?*

Since I spent much of my childhood abroad, both in the United States and in Hong Kong, I'd find myself more comfortable with Asian American or International students who had not spent their youth in Korea. Feeling like an outsider in my own country left me feeling a sense of emptiness that I've since overcome.

*1. What kind of child were you growing up and what were your interests?*

I was a people pleaser and strived to make my parents happy whenever possible. I was an extremely optimistic and outgoing kid who spent his childhood in Southern California and didn't really show any tell-tale signs I was academically inclined in any sense. When I moved back to Korea, I began to feel quite suffocated by the linear ranking system but things changed for the better again when I moved to Hong Kong where my parents placed me in an international school.

I adapted quickly to the project-based curriculum there and really enjoyed the emphasis that was placed on teamwork and creativity. For the first time in a long time, I embraced school life and found learning enjoyable. What was really surprising to me was that I eventually graduated as the valedictorian of my high school, getting straight A's throughout my four years. If you had asked me back in middle school that I would be ranked first in my high school, I never would have believed you since I never took my academics seriously as a kid.

Another memorable event in high school for me was scaling up the human rights club and being elected as President as a direct outcome of my efforts. I also was chosen to speak at a local TedX talk based on my work with the club. These early interests led me to earning a bachelor's degree in Policy Analysis and Management at Cornell University. Besides human rights, something that I was equally passionate about was mathematics. I gravitated towards the subject and even won first place at an international math competition. My love of math is what led me to my current major, Biostatistics at the T.H. Chan School of Public Health.

*2. How involved were your parents in helping you to prepare for Harvard? How did they help you to learn and grow?*

My parents were very attentive to my interests and needs and actively engaged in my academic success. Like most Korean families, there was an implicit understanding that school and academics were going to play an immense role in my future. My dad graduated from UCLA with an MBA, and had always wished I followed his steps and attended schools in the U.S. My dad would help me research different universities and majors, and my mom would actively help me connect with the right outlet of help or school that seemed most fitting for my interests and personality. They gave me the chance to go to SAT boot camps so that I could raise my score by 200. They found tutors for me in subjects that I needed a little extra help in. My dad would hand me a list of schools and majors I could look into.

This is not to say we did not have our moments of conflict when the situation tensed during this important college application process. I had moments where I burst out in tears, breaking down from stress.

Overall though, I felt supported by my parents, since they didn't pressure me to get into a certain school but helped me maximize my chances to seize opportunities by investing so much of their assets and resources (both monetary and non-monetary) to put me in Cornell and Harvard. Once they succeeded in putting me in Cornell, I found my own way to get into Harvard. I wasn't applying specifically to get into Harvard, but it ended up being my choice. My parents' ceaseless search for better tutors and programs was the driving force behind this.

*3. What is your most memorable memory in preparation for Harvard and what was something you experienced that you never thought you ever would?*

I studied Policy Analysis and Management at Cornell because I was interested in making large scale changes in the public. When you are studying policy, a core task of the field is measuring the effectiveness of the policy and gathering insights from past policies to improve.

In order to measure the effectiveness of policies, we utilized statistics. I had always loved math and had done well in it. I had started to uncover the realities of working in government and as a policy analyst. Without a country I could truly call my own, I began to doubt if I could start my career in this area. I was also starting to get disillusioned with the realities of how policies get implemented out in the real world. It seemed like a popularity contest. The policy that was admired by the crowd seemed to supersede the effective one. Ineffective yet widely-supported policies were the constant source of my frustration.

The more I dove deeper into practicing statistics in policy analyses, I realized I liked using numbers and analyzing them and the area of public health started to fascinate me. After I took more courses in public health policies, I knew I would still be able to positively contribute and impact the public through statistical analyses.

Later on, I gravitated more towards statistics, the tool needed to measure the effectiveness of the policies. Now I am doing my biostatistics program hoping I can use my passion and talent in statistics in a meaningful way. I am now striving to be a statistician in the realm of medical and/or pharmaceutical research.

*4. Study tips you have for younger students.*

I'd like to tell students to not take shortcuts in life. I've had college friends who found "clever" ways to get out of an exam, copy homework solutions from peers, and then tease me that I was the slow learner. But when you start developing dishonest habits like these in college, or even earlier than that, you're going to want to take the easy way out, cheat, and cut corners later on in life. You'll be presented with ample opportunities to take the easy way out. It'll get harder and harder to resist temptation then.

Make sure you tackle difficult situations head on, be authentic, and stay true to your core values.

If you take shortcuts at a young age, you're more likely to take shortcuts as an adult. Take responsibility and tackle difficult situations head on.

*5. What do you believe was your "X" factor to gain an admission to Harvard?*

For me, my Cornell degree helped me get into Harvard. I believe Harvard recognizes that students from Ivy Leagues or other top ranked schools are going to adjust well to Harvard. This could potentially help make up for the lack of experience in a specific field at the graduate level.

The second factor is a well-written personal statement. Both at the graduate level and the undergraduate level, it is critical to meaningfully present and tie your experiences to the admissions committee.

Another insight I can provide on the graduate school personal statement would be that it should be very clear and direct. Show the school the research you've done on the program and a detailed outline of the career opportunities you expect to pursue afterwards. This will leave the admissions office with the impression, "This student knows what they are doing and will do well here and even after they graduate." So, I think having a detailed, straightforward essay will work better over a fancy statement, obscured with impressive vocabulary.

*6. What are some of the challenges you have faced in school?*

Being in college and graduate school is one of the first times you're away from your parents. If you come from a family like mine who was so heavily involved with my upbringing, it may be slightly difficult to adjust to the fact that the ones giving you the most influence over your decisions will be your peers rather than your parents. With so much unstructured time, it's easy to feel a bit lost—so it's important to find a group of friends that can support you mentally.

*7. What do you find most valuable about your Harvard education?*

The School of Public Health is located in Boston, alongside the medical school and dental school. The school's agenda and schedule are more aligned with those of the medical school. One of the advantages of the school is the intimate relationship we share with these institutions. Obviously, anything public health related requires a lot of medical doctors because any epidemiological or statistical study would require medical expertise in public health studies. When we have events, seminars, or talks, we are usually going to have some people in the medical community. In terms of the school majors, I believe they are nine departments and three majors within the biostatistics department—Health Data Science, Biostatistics and Computational Biology & Quantitative Genetics.

The difference between the School of Public Health and the medical school is that most of what you know about your body, health prevention, or health policies comes from schools of public health and not from the medical school. For instance, if there's a study about whether a mask is effective in preventing infectious disease or not, it's probably from the School of Public Health.

As the School of Public Health is closely related to medical school, most of the student body are former doctors. A lot of the doctors come here either to rest, in between the medical school or to get their MPH, Master of Public Health. We have a small community in terms of the major—four biostatisticians and 20 people in our cohort. We're all really tightly knit because of the size of our cohort.

Our school is also filled with incredible faculty members. My favorite professor here, Professor Brent Coull, is incredibly renowned in the realm of statistics—a confidence interval that performs very well in binomial data is named after him. We also have famous scholars who also have a legacy in founding companies in public health. .

There's a lot of research opportunities once you get here. We are invited to events and career opportunities that have an inclination to hire Harvard students. We are also surrounded by incredible peers, faculty, and resources.–It is a great place that opens doors and builds those connections.

*8. What are you currently doing now or plan on doing in the future?*

I'm currently doing research as well as working as a teacher's assistant for two courses. My research project is focused on the effect of temperature on birth outcomes in women in Botswana. We want to understand the relationship between temperature and the pregnant woman and their infants. We only have eighteen temperature monitors around the country, but we'd like to have accurate temperature measurements representing the entire nation so we are relying on data points to estimate the entire country's average temperature every week from 2014 to 2019. The lack of resources and the creativity involved to utilize data makes it an interesting project.

In terms of a future career, I would really like to work in a hospital or pharmaceutical company or some sort of company that provides some beneficial service to the people. This can even be a product that will do just this. Ideally, I'd like to be involved in the data analysis side, and I just want to do statistically sound analysis that does not deceive the public in any way shape or form.

*Summary of Key Points:*

1. For Students: For your graduate school applications, make sure to research the program thoroughly and within your statement of purpose essay, write a detailed outline of your future career plans and how the program can help you achieve this.
2. For Parents: Your child may not show that he or she is academically inclined throughout childhood but trust in their abilities to succeed later on if they have the full support of their parents.
3. Look into the curriculum and learning models of the K-12 schools a student is enrolled in. Some students thrive under project-based curriculums, homeschooling, blended learning models, etc. In David's case, he started to enjoy school and learning once he switched over to the project-based curriculum during his high school years.

*Review:*

For David, he never dreamed in a million years that he would graduate as valedictorian of his high school class since he was not serious about academics when he was younger. David reminds us that it is never too late to find out what you are interested in. It may take a "spark" moment such as a change of environment, a change of schools, or an award at a competition that can make all the difference.

# The Investment Banker & Third Culture Kid

## Jill Seong

**Education:**
Harvard Kennedy School, Master in Public Administration, Class of 2020
The Wharton School, University of Pennsylvania, Master of Business Administration, Class of 2020
Cornell University, Bachelor of Arts in Economics, Class of 2013

**Working Experience:**
Goldman Sachs Investment Banking Associate

**Hometown:**
South Korea/Shanghai

This is a tough question for me because I'm more like a third culture kid. I moved out of Korea when I was five. My parents' home is still in Shanghai, but culturally, I would identify myself very strongly as being Korean. So, when someone asks me, "Where are you from?" I would answer Korea, but I also don't have much ties to Korea.

*What are your quirks? What do you think makes you unique?*

One of my quirks is that I have a near-obsession having to complete what I started, and in its fullest form, however silly. For example, when reading a book, I have to read front to back—including all the acknowledgments and the blurb at the back of the cover—to feel like I have really "read" the book.

Similarly, when I was really young, I woke up one morning with a strong urge to learn how to bike without training wheels. I knocked on my neighbor's door without hesitation, borrowed a bike from a girl a few years older than me, and spent close to half a day riding and falling on my own until I could ride it. By the time I returned home, my mom was worried sick because I was gone for a while, and my legs were bruised and bleeding from all the falls.

Another fun fact about me is that I have traveled to over 52 countries in my lifetime.

*1. What kind of child were you growing up, and what were your interests?*

In kindergarten, I used to play with a toy coin in the same corner of the room every day. I think the way my mom put it was that my concentration levels were through the roof even at that age. But I would also say, because I was so introverted, in retrospect, reading became my most predominant pastime because it was my lens of seeing the world from where I was most comfortable in.

I learned how to read and write in Korean when I was just two-years-old. By the end of early elementary school, I was reading books like *Jane Eyre* and *Wuthering Heights* and other "mature" books. But what's interesting about it is that even with books I've initially read in English or Chinese which I could have read in their original forms, I just strongly preferred to read them in Korean.

I read a lot of classics, and for books that I really liked, I read them about ten to fifteen times. And in some ways, I think I just have a very addictive personality. I'm not sure what it is exactly. So, by the time high school came around, many of the books we had to read for AP Literature class, I had read them all already and so many times too.

Besides reading, another interest of mine was drawing, but of two particular kinds.

After I finished a book, one of my favorite things to do was to immediately take out my sketchbook and draw the characters, in the way I pictured them as I read them. More often than not, they turned out very different from the characters portrayed in the film versions of the books. My drawing of Cho Chang from Harry Potter is a perfect example of this. I also loved to draw floor plans of the future house I would live in. I think I was heavily influenced by my parents at the time, who had just gotten into real estate investing and always took us on housing tours. These floor plans were pretty elaborate for a kid— detailed layout of bedrooms, bathrooms, indoor pools, amenities, etc., not just for my immediate family but also one for every aunt and uncle (yes, back then, I was innocent enough to think all my extended family would live in one massive "town")

My mom still has all of my twenty to thirty sketchbooks at her place. Even years later, I still find joy in these drawings from my childhood.

In terms of how I developed my personality from that shy little kid in the corner to a girl with more confidence, the change happened once our family moved to Shanghai so my dad could start his own business. Kids at international schools often move somewhere else after one or two years because of the nature of their parents' jobs. However, I had the advantage of continuing in the same school while there were lots of rotations for most other students. This familiarity gave me a lot of confidence. I also think the fact that I picked up sports along the way gave me a boost. In middle school, I picked up soccer and Kumdo martial arts. My mom also made my brother and I play tennis. All these sports paid off in the end.

*2. How involved were your parents in helping you to prepare for Harvard? How did they help you to learn and grow?*

One thing we did pretty well as a family was that we always had dinner together, or at least we tried to. Even if dad wasn't around because of work, my mom would sit down with us and have dinner.

And as part of that, you know, she would naturally talk about her childhood as a way to find topics to talk about over dinner. But I think it was very inspirational just hearing stories from her because she was a first-generation college student. She was attending Hanyang University in Seoul, but she lived an hour and a half away from the school, and since she didn't have any money, she would actually walk both ways every day. Even during the cold Korean winters, she did this and lived off only one pair of pants.

Just hearing all these stories from her and juxtaposing that with my somewhat privileged life made me realize that the life I was living was hard-earned. What I thought came easy to me was all because of the foundations that my parents worked tirelessly to build for us.

Another thing that struck me about my parents when I was a kid was that my parents couldn't speak any Chinese when we first moved to China. What they did was they got a tutor to come in every morning at 6 a.m. before my dad went to work. Both my mom and dad learned Chinese together every morning for an hour before my dad went off to work with the same Chinese tutor for seven years in a row. It's not only impressive that my dad was able to pull that off because of his work schedule but for my mom too. She was a homemaker, but she has always been a very intellectually curious woman, and she sat down every morning for every single class. They are both really good at Chinese now.

Although he worked long hours working for a Korean conglomerate, my dad made a considerable effort to make sure we went on family trips at least twice a year since my brother and I were little. So, we were hitting up places like Turkey and Israel. Even though it was from a privileged perspective, it made me realize that I live in a bubble and that there's so much to the world.

*3. What is your most memorable memory in preparation for Harvard, and what was something you experienced that you never thought you ever would?*

The way my application to Harvard worked was that I got into Wharton, and during my first semester at Wharton, I applied to Harvard Kennedy School, so it was almost like an add-on as a dual degree. And since I have to apply for a semester at Wharton, that also happened to be my busiest semester because I had to recruit for summer internships. I was doing investment banking recruiting, so I was really busy, literally going to New York City, three to four times a week.

When it came to the actual meat of the work in writing my application to Harvard, it was pretty last minute and probably not recommended for any future applicant out there. But in general, in preparing for Harvard, what was surprising to me during the process was I actually had a lot of clarity with my narrative in a way that I never had when I was applying to Cornell or Wharton. Because one thing I learned from my college application was, though this might sound super arrogant, Cornell wasn't my top undergraduate choice when it came to college applications, and that ended up being the best choice I had. I have what I want and obviously had a great time. But I think that process allowed me to understand the importance of creating a compelling narrative as part of your application.

When I was applying to Wharton, I spent a lot of time doing that. So that was a process that I went through with, so by the time the Harvard application was due, I felt like I already did a lot of the groundwork to start the application right away.

As I remember it, the application for Harvard was due at 5 p.m., and I started working on it at 5 a.m. The day before the due date, I had spent the entire night writing my investment banking interests and then moved onto working on the application.

*4. Study tips you have for younger students.*

For this, I will use an answer that I gave during a lecture to students. One of my aunts in Korea owns an English language academy, and she wanted me to come in for a day to do a quick lecture for the kids. These aren't a set of tactical study tips I gave to the students because they will hear adults tell them that they should have a specific dream and know what you want to become in the future, and these dreams should be the motivation for studying hard. This is especially prevalent in Korean culture, I would say. But I do feel like this discourages a lot of students sometimes. Many of them say that they don't have a dream yet, and it's not that crazy for a fourteen or sixteen-year-old today because you formulate your dreams based on knowledge and experience, and they haven't experienced all that much yet.

The second thing in terms of attitude towards studying is something my parents instilled in me.

They said that studying is not about whether I like it or not. To live somewhere, to become someone, there are certain responsibilities and roles you have to take because of who you are or your role in the family. The moment you decide not to do certain things because you do not feel like it, immediately leads to a breakage in the system. It's not like my dad one day wakes up and says I don't feel like going to work anymore. I don't feel like earning money for the family anymore. It's almost not an option. So, the same principle applies to study, they said. Having the choice to say I don't or want to do something is a luxury and working hard in school is not a luxury.

Although I am Christian, one of my favorite public figures is a Buddhist monk named Venerable Buhp Ryun, and I will never forget what he said during a seminar I had a chance to attend in person. To a troubled participant seeking advice on not being motivated enough in life, he said there is value to "just doing" things without complaints. Without the stress of not feeling motivated enough or enjoying enough, sometimes it's those very efforts to seek motivation that bar you from being motivated.

5. *What do you believe was your "X" factor in gaining admission to Harvard?*

Another thing I learned from my undergraduate level admissions process was the importance of recommendations. I had great and lovely teachers in high school, and they tried to write excellent recommendations for me. But at the end of the day, they are a substantial part of your entire package, so their narrative needs to match yours. So I think it's crucial to discuss how you are trying to portray yourself in your applications with your recommender. Let them know of at least three main traits you're trying to shine the spotlight on, to the extent that they agree, of course.

Another thing that I think worked for me in my graduate school applications was the understanding that as much as your recommenders love you and are there for you, they can't remember every single detail. So what I did was provide them with examples to jog their memories. I literally came up with a menu of examples to show them. I wasn't forcing them to use any of these examples, but it served more like a gentle reminder of my past achievements.

6. *What are some of the challenges you have faced in school?*

The greatest challenge I had at Harvard, not specifically because it was Harvard, but it just so happened that I was at a stage in my life where I was questioning my sense of identity. I never really grew up in China, nor did I go to school in Korea, but culturally identified myself as Korean. Back at Cornell, I somehow shied away from Korean students and made a more active effort to hang out with American kids to acclimate to the culture faster. So when I came to Wharton, one of the things that I wanted to change was to get to know more Korean students, but the first Korean gathering was very intimidating for me because there's a specific way you have to address people older than you and you also need to remember by how much older they are than you, and so on.

So when I came to Harvard Kennedy School, I joined the creative caucus of the Korean gateway program and served on the board. This made me interact with many Korean international students, and I realized people were surprisingly forgiving. I'm sure I made lots of mistakes at first when it came to communication, but everyone was kind and patient with me.

*7. What do you find most valuable about your Harvard education?*

I think I can talk about Harvard in general. So one thing, my dad said, after I told him that I got into Harvard Kennedy was that, for the first time, he was able to tell his friends and family about my recent admission without any additional explanation. Of course, Cornell and UPenn Wharton are exceptional schools, but in some parts of Korea, many people have not heard of Cornell or Wharton. But everyone knows Harvard. No other explanation is needed.

Relative to Cornell or Wharton, I think my experience at Harvard is apparent in the quality of speakers that come through. Ban Ki-Moon came two years ago. The president of this country or the prime ministers come in to speak to the students. That's a different caliber of speakers from the type of people that Wharton invited to speak, many of whom were corporate-specific and not top personalities of the nation.

*8. What are you currently doing or plan on doing in the future?*

I just started my second week at Goldman Sachs. So obviously, this will be my short term. But I've come to realize that the work and life balance will be way more important, and I'm not too sure how investment banking will come into play in that.

The summer before college, I put together a list of annual goals from 2009 up to 2040, writing down everything from when I wanted to get my MBA, when I wanted to achieve this and that, and the likes. In the long term, I want to establish schools in the developing world, specifically in China or Southeast Asia. This is a little more specific to China, as there is a phenomenon called 'left-behind children.' It is when many rural immigrants move to urban areas for work and leave their kids behind. Some are with grandparents, but many are left completely alone, and they have to go to school by themselves and come back home to try and take care of themselves. I want to improve the coverage of the school system, and I was hoping my Harvard education would give me more clarity on this issue, but I'm still trying to work things out.

*Summary of Key Points:*

1. For Students: It is okay if you are at a stage where you are not sure what to pursue for the future. Only time, observations, and experiences will help you make a decision. But in the meantime, the best thing you can do for yourself is to continue doing well in school as a solid educational foundation will be the springboard to launch your dream once you decide.

2. For Parents: Reminding students that studying is not a luxury, but a part of their responsibility can make them realize the value of education and how vital it can be to later help them achieve the goals that they have for themselves.

3. For your recommenders for college applications, let them know of your three strongest traits to make sure the narratives align. Draw up a list of your past achievements for them as a gentle reminder of the individual and student you were in the past.

*Review:*

Jill started out as an introvert who would play with the same toys and repeatedly reread the same books as a form of familiarity and comfort. Growing up, she watched her dad work tirelessly for the family and listened to stories of how her mother went through the hardships of being a poor first-generation college student. That motivated Jill to work hard and to never take her privileged life for granted. Her "doer" mentality and learning by example from her parents' actions, helped her gain admission to the top universities and as well blossom in the field of finance.

# The Computational Designer & Language Enthusiast

## Eunsu Kim

**Education:**
Harvard Graduate School of Design, Master in Landscape Architecture & Master in Design Studies, Technology, Class of 2020
University of Seoul, Bachelor's Degree in Landscape Architecture

**Working Experience:**
Samsung C&T Assistant Manager

**Hometown:**
Gwangju, South Korea

*What are your quirks? What do you think makes you unique?*

I am passionate about learning new things and new experiences.

*1. What kind of child were you growing up and what were your interests?*

Curiosity has always been my nature as a kid. I was especially drawn to how computers work and the idiosyncrasies of languages. I remember when I was fifteen-years-old, I bought gadgets, widgets, parts, and pieces to assemble a computer of my very own. I just had to know the groundwork of how it functioned to satisfy my curiosity. When I wasn't building machines from scratch, I loved learning new languages, finding joy in trying to imitate the pronunciation and intonations of other languages. It wasn't enough for me to watch foreign movies and dramas dubbed in Korean. I wanted to experience and understand the films in the original language so besides English, I studied Chinese and Japanese on my own. In my everyday affairs, I would try to form words and sentences in a different language in my head and ask myself, "What was this word in Japanese again?" and repeated it until it was fully ingrained in my head. Looking back, my tendency to know the foundations of subjects carried on to reflect who I am today. My dedication to my studies enabled me to graduate from the Harvard Graduate School of Design with two master's degrees.

*2. How involved were your parents in helping you to prepare for Harvard? How did they help you to learn and grow?*

My decision to prepare for Harvard almost seemed like a last-minute decision to my parents when in hindsight, I just wanted to make sure this was what I wanted. In my case, I was working for a set time before I finally found the urge to study and to gain new experiences. My parents didn't have much input or influence with me choosing to study abroad for my graduate studies, but once they found out I was putting together my applications, they were extremely supportive of my decision. Due to this support, I was able to go abroad to Harvard with a peace of mind knowing that I had the absolute trust and support of my parents.

*3. What is your most memorable memory in preparation for Harvard and what was something you experienced that you never thought you ever would?*

The reason I decided to leave my job was ultimately, I started to question my identity without the Samsung title under my name. Say that one day the company closes its business or that I leave the company, I wondered if I could make it out there on my own with my backpack of tools. Although I may have been working at a prominent and reputable company, I realized that I, myself, was lacking in the skill sets needed to truly survive on my own if the case were to happen.

During my career at Samsung, I was in charge of the last stage of projects such as construction management. I had always wanted to work on the earlier and creative stages of the projects instead of wrapping up the finishing touches. Although it was a part of my job to improve the design at the construction site through implementation, I wanted to contribute to the developmental and ideation process. Once I wanted a change in my daily career life, that's when thoughts of attending graduate school to gain new knowledge and skillsets came to mind.

At first, I went for a master's degree in Landscape Architecture. I learned how to design for open spaces. I wanted to try incorporating technology into these designs to enhance the experience of those who would be interacting with space. I didn't want to work in the conventional design field so I became more interested in how to utilize data for urban analytics and the future of cities.

When I first came to the States, there were challenges that I never thought that I would have or encounter. The cultural differences, the change of surroundings, and the fact that I was away from my family and friends were not something that I was used to. However, this feeling did not last too long as I quickly adjusted to the new environment that was teeming with diversity and gave me so much inspiration for my design projects.

*4. Study tips you have for younger students.*

I think it is crucial to be able to create your original story. When I first arrived at Harvard, I noticed a lot of my peers had come to graduate school with a degree in architecture already under their belt from their years at undergrad. But, I, on the other hand, had slightly steered away from my initial career path so it was essential for me to create a story that explained why I made this decision. Even during the process of finding that story, I was able to think hard about what I wanted to study, what I wanted to do afterward, and why it was important to me. As I deeply dug into research about the field and even within myself, I began to grow more passionate and committed to the field I chose. Finding one's own story is my greatest advice to any student applying to universities.

*5. What do you believe was your "X" factor to gain admission to Harvard?*

As a joke, my friend and I would always say how Harvard's admission committee made a big mistake and let me in.

Jokes aside, if I were to evaluate my application, I think my past work experience was what helped me out the most. One of the biggest things I felt was that there is much more appreciation for having various experiences here in the U.S. In Korea, however, if people know that someone has decided to switch fields, many believe that person is just, "wasting all that time and effort away." Let's say you were doing music for years and suddenly one day, wanted to drop your instrument and music sheets on the ground to pursue a degree in architecture. Many in Korea would scorn your decision and urge you to stay on the path that you were on originally. But the people I have met here tend to advocate for interdisciplinary learning and see value in the incorporation of various experiences.

Since my work experience was construction management at the construction site, I think it intrigued the admission officers to see me combine my past work experience with my major of choice.

Another critical element in my applications that deserves much credit is that I received a lot of help from those around me when I applied. My colleagues at work, and my study group members all helped me with the greatest intentions. As I started to prepare for the application, people seemed to appear in the right place and the right time to help me. I would not be here today without their help. There were a lot of people who helped me without expecting anything in return. When I think about it now, I think it was because they saw how hard I was working towards this goal and how much I wanted it.

*6. What are some of the challenges you have faced in school?*

I had always thought I was the type to easily adapt to new environments, but it was still difficult to live in an entirely different place.

Initially, English and language barriers were a struggle for me, but something that hit me, even more, was constantly competing with insanely bright individuals in one place. If someone was accomplished enough to get into Harvard, they were most likely the big fish of their pond. However, once I arrived here at Harvard, I couldn't stop feeling like the small fish in the pond.

The design school building is designed in the shape of stairs, so you can see everyone's work. You get inspired by all the work as you traverse up and down these "stairs" but it can get a bit overwhelming at times looking at the sheer talent displayed on the walls. In the end, it turned out to be a great opportunity to present my work to other cohorts, share each other's thoughts, and find a way to collaborate with others, which is the best experience at the school despite all the challenges.

*7. What do you find most valuable about your Harvard education?*

Harvard in general allows its students to cross-register with MIT so it provided me with a lot of freedom to be able to take whatever classes I wanted to. The design school also had close ties with Harvard's business school, law school, or education school, which was helpful for me to broaden my insight and network.

Another thing is that Harvard is rich in resources, so it provides an environment where you can accomplish anything if your goals are clear. There are world-class experts all over the school that you could work with, and you can take advantage of any resources that the school is providing. Also, because you are a Harvard student, even if you could email someone about your thesis and ask them for some help, there will be people who would be willing to get to know more about your research and thought process.

*8. What are you currently doing now or plan on doing in the future?*

I'm not the type to live on a scheduled plan. Instead, I tend to live life spontaneously. Of course, I will continue to move forward with my interests and goals as my 'keywords' in life. I want to keep building my experience in the U.S. and further explore my interests. In other words, I will think of life as if it was a sentence where my 'keywords' and newly found words can be added to the sentence along the way. If Harvard helped me find my field of keywords, I have yet to make the sentences with them. That is why I plan to gain this knowledge through hands-on experience in the professional field.

*Summary of Key Points:*

1. For Students: Many believe that college applications are a solo activity, but there will be friends, peers, and family members around you who will be willing to offer insight and help if they see that you desire to attend a certain university.
2. For Parents: Once students arrive at college, it will be easy for them to compare themselves to their peers in both abilities and accomplishments. Remind them that everybody has their strengths and to utilize their strength in their field of study.
3. Although working at a top, reputable company is admirable and coveted by many, stop to ask yourself if you could sustain a living on your one if one day, the company shuts down for various reasons.

*Review:*

Eunsu not only thought about what program she was interested in for her graduate studies, but she also let the location and diversity of the location drive her decision to drive her decision on which universities to apply for. Although she was at first intimidated by her peers and their accomplishments, she quickly changed her perspective to see that all of her classmates were sources of inspiration and designers to collaborate on projects with. She encourages applicants who have various interests or feel the need to completely change majors or career paths to find countries that promote interdisciplinary learning.

# The Aspiring Lawyer & (Now) Fan of Television

## Jin Lee

**Education:**
Harvard Law School, Class of 2022
Dartmouth College, Bachelor of Arts in Mathematics and Classical Languages and Literature
British School of Kuwait, Hanyoung Foreign Language High School

**GPA and Test Scores:**
Hanyoung Foreign Language High School GPA, (4.7+/4)
SAT I, (2400)
SAT II, (Physics (800), Biology (800), Chemistry (800), Math 2C (800))
APs, (French (4), Calculus BC (5), US History (5), Biology (5), Chemistry (5), Physics B (5), Physics C E&M (5), Physics C Mechanics (5), Psychology (5), Environmental Studies (5))
GRE, (169)

**Extracurriculars and Awards:**
Internship at Yonsei Severance Hospital, President of School Photography Club

**Hometown:**
Hanover, New Hampshire

*What are your quirks? What do you think makes you unique?*

I started watching TV and playing *Pokémon Go* only after I started law school.

*1. What kind of child were you growing up and what were your interests?*

I grew up in the Middle East for most of my childhood, (Kuwait and the United Arab Emirates, specifically) and I was basically moving every three years because of my parents' jobs. I had gone to six schools within six years. It was a lot of adjusting for a small kid.

I moved to the Middle East when I was five as a Korean citizen and didn't really speak any English. My parents placed me at an international school and I had a really good time there because all the kids were just like me. Then, when I came back to Korea, everybody there treated me like a foreigner upon finding out that I grew up abroad. They treated me as Korean, in a way, but as someone who had vastly different experiences than their own, so I had to adjust again when I came back. For part of my personal statement for law school, I wrote about how I learned to adapt to different cultures quickly. Most law school personal statements are pretty formulaic: you talk about who you are and why you think you will make a good lawyer. In mine, I said that I learned to listen really well, since I found myself in so many different cultural situations that I had to learn by listening. I connected this with my point that, as a lawyer, you have to really listen to your client's needs to find out the solution.

*2. How involved were your parents in helping you to prepare for Harvard? How did they help you inspire you to learn and grow?*

So, surprisingly, not hands-on.

They were very relaxed about everything. I think one thing my dad did emphasize was the opportunities that were out there for me and I think that motivated me. When I was in high school, he would just say really casually, "I heard that this college is a great school or even this one…" My mom was also really supportive of whatever I wanted to do. So when I told them I wanted to attend college in the U.S., they were really surprised because they thought I would just attend college in Korea. I convinced them that I could make it, and then, after that, they were completely on board with me. Even in high school, when everybody was staying in school for ten hours a day, I left early on some days just to go practice ballet, and that was totally okay with them.

I'll also answer this question in a slightly different way. I have two younger brothers, and my parents were a bit different with how they handled them. When I was young, my parents would help me solve my math problems, but for my brothers, they became more relaxed and it was even more of a hands-off approach. One of my brothers wanted to be a professional soccer player, and my parents gave him the clear. It didn't really work out for him, but he is in graduate school now studying international relations. He wrote for his personal statement that soccer was a dream he pursued, and even though it didn't happen for him, it was okay. He learned a lot of great things during the process of pursuing his passion, and this was how he found out he wanted to pursue international relations, instead. For parents, I think it is helpful to let kids do whatever they are interested in, to an extent, because kids don't really know what they want to do if they are constantly being told what they should do.

*3. What is your most memorable memory in preparation for Harvard and what was something you experienced that you never thought you ever would?*

So, I'm going to talk about both college and law school. When I made the decision to change my major to Classics, I took this Latin class and I found myself reading Latin in its original form—it was so surreal. This was something that I thought I would never experience. The reason why I decided to be a Classics major was because of something my writing professor said during my first year of college, "Your soul will not be complete until you've read this in the original." By the end of my senior year, I was reading Plato in ancient Greek.

Then, after my time at Dartmouth, I went on to become a consultant. I was working with businesses to help them achieve their goals, which can be good or bad depending on how you look at it. I found out that when you actually know the law, a lot of it depends on how you work with it. I was working with businesses going through restructuring, and there were a lot of lawyers working on the case. That's how I got inspired to become a lawyer. After that, I went to Algeria to not only work as a researcher, but because I needed time to prepare for the LSAT and get myself together for law school.

*4. Study tips you have for younger students.*

I think I have two things I did really well. I was good at discovering the "fun factor" of whatever it was I was doing, even for the things I did not like. During middle school, I really hated this one subject, but I had this gel pen that I really liked. So, I used this pen to take notes for this specific class. That gel pen helped me get through that class instead of dreading every single minute of it. I know it's silly and I wouldn't do it now, but back in middle and high school, it really worked for me. Another thing I did that really helped was making use of the downtime or free periods during school. It was called self-study time, and some kids used it to nap or to catch up with friends, but I used those 40 minutes to get as much homework done as possible.

I know this one is obvious, but after high school, I realized sleep is super important just to function as a human being. So now, I never stay up past midnight. This has made me super efficient during the day to complete everything on my to-do list. A lot of people think law students stay up late hours into the night reading case studies, but I can tell you a lot of law students don't ever stay up past midnight.

*5. What do you believe was your "X" factor to gain an admission to Harvard?*

I think, for Harvard Law School (and for any law school in the U.S., really), it's a game of whether or not you have a great GPA and LSAT score. For your personal statement, since the law professors read it, if you don't come across as somebody who is very obnoxious, then they won't reject you. If you seem like a genuine and respectful student, then they will take your application very seriously. So, it comes down to how you maintain your GPA and LSAT score.

As for my undergraduate admission to Dartmouth, I think my interview went well. You really want to showcase your strengths and what you can do to your interviewer. I remember one of my interview questions was, "What do you think of Google cache?" His spiel was that his kids were arguing on Facebook and that Google cache was saving everything that they were saying. He then asked me what are the ramifications of privacy and what I thought about it. His last question for me was what I liked to do for fun as a high school student, and I said that I read Wikipedia articles. To this, he remarked, "Well, how do you know that they're true?" I answered that I check my sources.

For your personal statement for college, as a high schooler, you may be at a stage where you are not that certain about everything yet. But, if you know your strengths and weaknesses and emphasize what is unique about you, your personal statement will be one of the strongest elements in your application.

*6. What are some of the challenges you have faced in school?*

I'll talk about two challenges. The first challenge was actually back in high school. Just getting a sense of self. I think I should have known that I didn't share the same experiences as the other Korean students in my school. All the kids came from the same neighborhood and grew up together. I should have realized that people come from different backgrounds and upbringings and that all stories deserve respect. But, I never told people that I grew up abroad in the Middle East. I just told them that I was from the neighborhood too, just because I didn't want to answer any of their questions. Looking back, I could have handled that much better and just could have been proud of the differences that set me apart.

One other challenge that I am facing currently(actually, a lot of people are facing right now) is being judged because of your gender or race. Hopefully, this will change. I think it is especially hard to be respected if you are a woman or a person of color in certain industries. So, for example, this came from a Harvard professor, but I told him that I went to Dartmouth as an undergraduate and he was like, "Really?" His reaction just made me feel like I didn't deserve the education that I received. I know it seems like nothing, but it happens pretty often to a lot of my peers too.

*7. What do you find most valuable about your Harvard education?*

My classmates and the guest speakers that Harvard invites, some of whom I've met in person. I learn a lot from these speakers, as well as my own peers. The fact that it is Harvard Law School means that they have the ability to invite anybody from all walks of life and backgrounds. Former U.S. Secretary of State Madeleine Albright came in one day, and she was talking a lot about foreign policy and how, one evening, she had to invite the Prime Minister of Israel to her private home because she was trying to negotiate a deal. She also told us a fun story of a time her young granddaughter once said, "I don't see what the big deal is about Granny Maddie being Secretary of State." After Madeleine Albright, the next female Secretary of State was Condoleezza Rice. Then after her, it was Hillary Clinton. The moral of her story was that it only seems strange to the rest of the world when, for the first time, a woman takes on a position that is usually held by a man, but eventually, the change is accepted. That was a fun story to listen to, and I don't think I would have had access to that insight anywhere else.

Aside from the speakers that come in, as a law student, I actually enjoyed my first year. It's just a big final at the end of the semester. So you're just reading and studying for the semester, then, at the end of the semester, you take the exam. This was relaxing for me. As for the professors, they are surprisingly accessible, and they will actually play trivia with you. During the height of the pandemic, there was this one trivia match on Zoom and all the law professors decided to play trivia with us at seven in the evening.

In class, you have to be alert at all times. Law school is based on cases and cold calls. So, you read a case study and the case's decision, then you go to class. The professor doesn't lecture, but will call your name off of a list. Then, they will ask you about the facts of the case, or the reasoning of the case, or what you should learn about the case. I know that different professors have different styles. Some professors like to grill you for thirty minutes or some professors like to do what we call "popcorn style" and just jump around. But it's based on cases and it's based on cold calls. So you had better come prepared.

*8.What are you currently doing now or plan on doing in the future?*

Right now, I'm doing an internship with the World Bank. I'm working with the business team, which means I talk with contributors from around the world and try to find out whether there has been reform in the business sectors. If there are reforms, then I reflect that on the business report. After graduation, I would like to be like a bankruptcy or restructuring lawyer in New York City.

*Summary of Key Points:*

1. For Students: Discover the "fun factor" of whatever task is at hand. Even the ones that you dread. It may take an amazing gel pen or wearing your favorite sneakers to a class you hate to make the experience enjoyable.
2. For Parents, it is helpful to let kids do what they are interested in, to an extent. They may not know what they really want to do because they are constantly being told what they should do.
3. For law school applications, take the time to focus more on how you maintained your GPA and performed on your LSAT (Law School Admission Test).

*Review:*

Jin's story of how she adapted to so many different schools, homes, and cultures throughout her early life is a story some students can relate to. Especially those who have been uprooted more times than they can count. She also acknowledges, particularly for law school applications, the importance of having great scores, but also reminds readers and future law school applicants that they should portray themselves as genuine and honest individuals to be considered for admission.

# The Architect & Insect Enthusiast

## Hyunsuk Yun

**Education:**
Harvard Graduate School of Design, Master in Architecture, Class of 2020
Kookmin University

**GPA and Test Scores:**
GRE, (154/170/3.5)

**Extracurriculars and Awards:**

**Working Experience:**
*Internship experiences at architecture and landscape design firms in Korea. Construction site and document management experience while in military service.*

**Hometown:**
Seoul, South Korea

*What are your quirks? What do you think makes you unique?*

Instead of solely being involved in architecture, I have interests in other areas. Due to my array of interests, I find it easy to talk to anyone. When I first arrived in the U.S., my English was terrible, but I was still able to spark up a conversation with almost anybody. This ability came in handy throughout my time abroad.

*1. What kind of child were you growing up and what were your interests?*

I was a really stubborn child. I never ended up doing what people told me to do or even learn. As a matter of fact, I persistently resisted participating in the activities that were pushed upon me. I was simply not interested. I refused to take piano lessons, I quit swimming, and I never even learned Taekwondo. Those were considered some of the basic activities that most Korean parents made their children do. However, the activities that I found to be truly interesting were Korean traditional calligraphy, fine arts, and entomology.

I loved everything about bugs, back then. During that time, insects were the only thing on my mind. I remember spending my summer days with my insect collections. Looking back, I think I became fascinated by the diverse assortment of shapes and colors among insects, which still amazes me to this day. I was also really into painting and calligraphy at a young age, but also immersed myself in STEM subjects in high school, namely mathematics and biology. Once, I memorized the value of pi (3.14…) up to a thousand decimal places. Even now, I still remember up to 200 decimal places. When the time came to decide on a career path, I tried to find a field that encompasses both the artistic traits I had in my childhood and the scientific interests that I fostered during my high school years. Architecture was the perfect fit.

*2. How involved were your parents in helping you to prepare for Harvard? How did they help you to learn and grow?*

My parents were pretty open-minded compared to many other parents who had a strong say in their children's field of study and future career. My parents, on the other hand, never placed high expectations on me to go to Harvard, much less help me work towards that lofty goal . Nevertheless, I strongly believe that their sincere trust and support was what made every single step towards my Harvard education possible. They never doubted me, and always encouraged me to find my passions and pursue them.

*3. What is your most memorable memory in preparation for Harvard and what was something you experienced that you never thought you ever would?*

In order to apply for the Harvard Graduate School of Design, one of the three letters of recommendation needs to be written by someone who graduated with a degree in design. Though there was one professor I knew I could ask, we were not particularly close. So, the whole process of approaching the professor for a letter of recommendation felt quite complicated. Through this experience, I learned that I had to develop good relationships with my professors.

*4. Study tips you have for younger students.*

In Korea, students feel pressured to meet external standards and parents' wishes. For this reason, those students have trouble figuring out what it is that they really want for themselves. Most parents tell their children to work hard in order to get good grades, but fail to teach them the importance of relationship skills or of developing career paths.

Finding out what you like actually takes a lot of time and effort. Because this process is so open-ended, it may seem difficult at first. However, I think it's time well spent to seek interests that will inform one's career path. Just studying won't do.

*5. What do you believe was your "X" factor to gain an admission to Harvard?*

Each applicant to the Harvard Graduate School of Design is required to submit a portfolio that showcases his or her architectural, artistic, and academic potential. This portfolio is the most important factor for admission to the GSD. I think the architectural work in my portfolio was special in terms of the different techniques and approaches that most architecture students would not have demonstrated at the undergraduate level. I think my original style strengthened my application the most. Also, my portfolio showed how I engaged with the "design thinking" process. In other words, instead of being fixated on the final product, I was more mindful of the process of creating something through refinement and development.

*6. What are some of the challenges you have faced in school?*

In Korea, people are raised to suppress their thoughts and opinions. Though I thoroughly enjoyed America's open-discussion culture, I also found it quite difficult to adjust to. Moreover, I came in with a background in architectural design, but others came in with backgrounds in architectural history or engineering, so they used jargon that was foreign to me. Another struggle was the language barrier itself. I would often miss out on culture-specific references scattered throughout conversations.

*7. What do you find most valuable about your Harvard education?*

I personally think that Harvard is the best architectural school in the world. Of the many reasons as to why I think this is the case, one is the unlimited resources at the institution. Harvard has a deep pocket of research funds, in addition to a high reputation, so students have the resources to move forward with any idea for a project.

If we are talking about the Graduate School of Design, specifically, becoming an architect doesn't guarantee that you will make huge earnings through your work. Generally speaking, the field of architecture requires us to be highly educated, work long hours, and gives us unbelievably low pay. So, a lot of architecture schools and programs around the world generally do not have enough funding to offer their students, which, in turn, limits the students' creativity to reach its full potential. So, the "unlimited resources," such as the latest cutting-edge technology, provided by Harvard's GSD program means a lot to all of the architecture students here. There are very few programs out there that can do the same.

This idea of being "limitless" really hit me once I arrived in the U.S. In comparison, the education I received in Korea felt quite restraining; only a handful of career paths seemed feasible for students. However, I was able to escape such restrictions at Harvard, and was granted full creative liberty. This freedom is the best part of education here.

*8. What are you currently doing now or plan on doing in the future?*

I am currently planning on staying in Boston to work as a Junior Architect, but I think I'll have to think about what specifically I will do in the future. My former work experiences in Switzerland and France broadened my perspective on architecture and construction, so either of those places could be my next destination to pursue my career in the coming years. Studying architecture and becoming an architect takes a long time. Even when you are forty or fifty-years-old, you are considered as a "young" professional in the field, as it takes time to establish a name for yourself. Those with a design degree from Harvard are no exception.

*Summary of Key Points:*

1.  For Students: When putting together a design portfolio, instead of just focusing on the end product, highlight your design thinking process for each piece in the portfolio. This will demonstrate that you place value in creating something through refinement, development, and iterations.
2.  For Parents: Students should not only focus on academics in school, but should be encouraged to take the time to get to know their teachers. A strong endorsement or recommendation letter from a trusted teacher can play a crucial role in admission to a certain school.
3.  One of the benefits of attending the Harvard Graduate School of Design are the unlimited resources. The students are equipped with the materials needed, including the latest technology, to move forward with any creative endeavor.

*Review:*

Hyunsuk's unyielding personality as a child to go against the "traditional path" led him to cultivate unique interests, namely entomology, calligraphy, and memorizing the values of pi up to a thousand decimal places. He reminds students that they may receive external pressure from parents and teachers to perform well or to meet certain expectations, but to not be overwhelmed by this pressure. Instead, he advises students to be in tune with what their true interests are, and how these interests can inform their career path.

www.ingramcontent.com/pod-product-compliance
Lightning Source LLC
Chambersburg PA
CBHW062050080426
42734CB00012B/2600